Computer Language Reference Guide

With Keyword Dictionary

by Harry L. Helms, Jr.

Howard W. Sams & Co., Inc.
4300 WEST 62ND ST. INDIANAPOLIS, INDIANA 46268 USA

Preface

Very often, people involved with computers find themselves confronted with programs that are written in languages other than those that they normally use or are familiar with. The result is often frustration. There are innumerable books detailing how to program in the various languages, but it is often a difficult task to extract the essentials of each language from such material. That is the void this book attempts to fill.

This is *not* a quickie guide to programming in the various computer languages. Programming cannot be taught in a book of this size. Rather, this is a "phrase book" for the "traveller" who is outside of the programming language normally used. This book assumes a working knowledge of one of the programming languages that is covered in it as well as a familiarity with the basic computer concepts. Also, it does not try to be the last definitive word for any of the languages covered; completeness has been sacrificed for conciseness and accessibility.

However, enough essentials have been included for each language so that, hopefully, you will be able to understand what is going on in a program that is written in a language you are not familiar with. This should be of a particular value if you must use "canned" software or if you wish to adapt a program written in another language to the one that you normally use. It should also be of value if you wish a broad overview of some of the most commonly used languages. It may also lead you to a better appreciation of the strengths and weaknesses of the various computer languages.

One major problem has been the numerous versions of each computer language that are available. In this book, an attempt has been made to focus on the most common versions of each language, although the bulk of the minor differences between versions of the same language had to be omitted. In cases where there are major differences between different versions, the reader has been referred to the system reference manual or programming guide.

Often languages are differently implemented on small systems versus large computer systems, with many of the differences coming in the input/output section (punch card as opposed to video terminal, for example). No attempt has been made to cover such differences here due to their complexity; again, consult the reference material for the system that the program is written for.

Naturally, each language will have its own features that cannot "translate" into other languages, such as BASIC's interactive features, Pascal's data-type flexibility, or COBOL's readability for the nonprogrammer. No human language can be translated word for word into another language and no program written in one computer language can be exactly transformed into another. You will have to compensate for this by using the features of the language that you normally use to the maximum advantage.

But, if you are a BASIC programmer who has been wondering what Pascal is all about, or if you are curious about the difference between a PL/1 and COBOL "picture," then this book is dedicated to you.

HARRY L. HELMS, JR.

Contents

chapter 1

ALGOL

Introduction

ALGOL (*Algo*rithmic *L*anguage) is the result of the joint efforts of an American organization known as the *Association for Computing Machinery* and a German society named *Gesellschaft fur Angewandte Mathematik und Mechanik*. In 1957, they began work on a language that could be internationally accepted by makers and users of computers. In 1958, the first version of ALGOL was introduced. Soon after its introduction, refinements were developed by John Backus for ALGOL and it became known as the Backus-Naur Form (BNF). Numerous other revisions were incorporated into a new version, ALGOL, that was introduced in 1962.

ALGOL has managed to achieve a wide acceptance and use in Europe but it has not achieved the same status in the United States. One major reason is that major hardware manufacturers have not supported ALGOL with the same enthusiasm that the other languages have enjoyed. In a large measure, this is because ALGOL, in its original form, required the use of symbols that were not commonly available on input/output devices. More serious were some of the problems inherent in the language. Its character-string handling abilities are so weak as to be almost nonexistent. Input and output statements are not an inherent part of the language but must be implemented through procedures. (Some standardized input and output procedures have since been developed for use with ALGOL.)

The recent explosion in mini- and microcomputers has brought about a renewed interest in all programming languages with the notable exception of ALGOL. While still used daily in programming, ALGOL seems to be rapidly on its way to becoming the Greek or Latin of computer languages—a "dead" language which managed to spawn others (most notably Pascal).

ALGOL Symbols

One of the greatest difficulties with ALGOL is, as was mentioned, the unusual symbols used. Many of these are not available on input/output hardware that is normally found in the United States. Two sets of alternative symbols, EBCDIC and BCD, have been developed in an attempt to ease these compatibility problems. Table 1-1 lists the "reference" ALGOL symbols along with their EBCDIC and BCD equivalents.

Table 1-1. ALGOL Symbols and EBCDIC/BCD Equivalents

Reference	EBCDIC	BCD
a ... z	A ... Z	A ... Z
0 ... 9	0 ... 9	0 ... 9
+ − X	+ − *	+ − *
/ ÷	/ '/'	/ '/'
↑	** or POWER	** or POWER
<, >	<, >	LESS, GREATER
≤, ≥	<=, =>	NOTGREATER, NOTLESS
=	=	= or EQUAL
¬	¬	NOT
≠	¬=	NOT EQUAL
. ,	. ,	. ,
: ;	: ;	.. .,
:=	:=	.= or ..=
( )	( )	( )
[ ]	(/ /)	(/ /)
$_{10}$ subscript	'	'

Program Format

Each ALGOL program starts with BEGIN and terminates with END. Remarks or comments that are not executed may be inserted into the program by COMMENT. All variables used in a program must be declared as to their type (real, integer, or Boolean) before being used in executed statements. The sequence of a typical ALGOL program is:

```
BEGIN
    variable type declarations
    executable statements or procedures
    comments as desired
END
```

Each statement in the ALGOL language ends with a semicolon (;). The exceptions are BEGIN and END.

Procedures are actually complete ALGOL programs contained within the body of a larger ALGOL program. Procedures are identified by the word PROCEDURE followed by the name of the procedure. Procedures start with BEGIN and terminate with END just as larger ALGOL programs do.

Normally, statements are not numbered or labeled in ALGOL. However, labels may be added for special purposes (this will be described later). Labels must begin with a letter and must be followed by a colon.

Some versions of ALGOL specify that keywords must be enclosed in single quotes, as in 'BEGIN', 'END', 'PROCEDURE', etc. Most versions of ALGOL used in the United States follow this convention; thus, it will be used here.

Variables and Arrays

In the ALGOL language, all variables must be declared before they can be used in the program. Variable declarations must follow 'BEGIN' and cannot follow any executable statement using the variables. As a general rule, only 'COMMENT' may precede the variable declarations.

Variables are declared using 'REAL' or 'INTEGER', as in these examples:

```
'INTEGER' AGE, DATE, CONST;
'REAL' TEMP, PI;
```

In addition, variables having the values of true and false may be declared using 'BOOLEAN':

```
'BOOLEAN' A, B;
```

Variable names can consist of any combination of letters and numbers so long as the first letter of the name is a letter. If two names have the same first six characters, they are treated as the same variable in ALGOL.

Arrays may be established by the proper declaration. The declaration

```
'REAL' 'ARRAY' NUMBER(/1:10/);
```

causes an array of NUMBER to be set up in steps of one and its indices will range from 1 to 10. The values of the array are real. Multidimensional arrays can be set up by adding other dimensions to the declaration and separating them by commas, as in:

```
'REAL' 'ARRAY' NUMBER(/1:10, 1:15/);
```

Arrays may be established of real, integer, or Boolean values. Sometimes an array may be declared by simply using 'ARRAY'. In such cases, all values in the array are automatically treated as real in the program.

Arithmetic Operations

In the ALGOL language, arithmetic operations are performed using the following symbols:

+	Addition
−	Subtraction
×	Multiplication
/	Real number division
÷	Integer number division
↑	Exponentiation
: =	Equals (result of an operation)

However, some implementations of ALGOL use a different set of symbols. These are given below:

+	Addition
−	Subtraction
*	Multiplication
/	Real number division
'/'	Integer number division
**	Exponentiation
: =	Equals (result of an operation)

Operations in ALGOL are performed in the following order:

1. Operations in parentheses, regardless of preceding and succeeding operators.
2. Exponentiation.
3. Multiplication and division.
4. Addition and subtraction.

Boolean Operators

ALGOL also includes Boolean operators that are used to compute true/false values. They are:

$\wedge$ And
$\vee$ Or
$\supset$ Implies
$\equiv$ Equivalent

When evaluating Boolean values, the operations are performed in the following order:

1. Arithmetic expressions as detailed earlier.
2. $<$, $\leq$, $=$, $\geq$, $>$, $\neq$
3. $\neg$
4. $\wedge$
5. $\vee$
6. $\supset$
7. $\equiv$

Constants

A constant may be established in ALGOL by first declaring a name for it, using the same steps by which variable names are declared. A constant value can then be assigned to the name by using the assignment symbol:

5 := CONSTANT

The symbol := is used to assign the value of a number, variable or constant, to another variable or constant. The symbol = is used with Boolean variables to indicate that the two variables are the same.

Conditional Expressions

There are several common conditional expressions in ALGOL, such as:

```
'IF' condition 'THEN' consequence
'IF' condition 'THEN' consequence 'ELSE' consequence
```

The condition in these statements is a Boolean expression that uses the following symbols:

```
=, <, >, ⌐=, <= (≤), >=(≥)
```

The consequence of these statements may be a numerical value, a variable name, a label, or another conditional expression. It is also possible to determine the value of a variable using a conditional expression and the assignment symbol:

```
SUM := 'IF' condition 'THEN' 1 'ELSE' 0;
```

In this statement, the value of SUM will be either 1 or 0 depending upon the condition.

A loop may be established in ALGOL using a 'FOR' statement. The two most common 'FOR' statements are:

```
'FOR' condition 'STEP' index value 'UNTIL' ending value 'DO' action
'FOR' condition 'WHILE' condition 'DO' action
```

The first 'FOR' statement will cause an action to be repeated for a finite number of times. The loop begins at the condition following 'FOR' and repeats until it reaches the value following 'UNTIL'. The count toward the value following 'UNTIL' increases each time the action is performed by the increment that follows 'STEP'. The second 'FOR' statement allows for indefinite repetition of the loop as long as the condition following 'WHILE' is met. A single execution can be caused by simply omitting 'WHILE'.

Unconditional Expressions and Labels

Although statement labels are not required in ALGOL, they may be used as needed for unconditional expressions. A statement may be labeled in the following manner:

```
LABEL: statement
```

In this example, LABEL is the label that applies to the statement following it. The label could be any other name that follows the same general rules applying to variable names. Note that labels are *not* enclosed in single quotes.

Labeled statements are often used with the unconditional transfer-of-control statement 'GO TO', as in this example:

'GO TO' LABEL;

which causes execution of the program to immediately shift to the statement identified by LABEL.

There is a special form of *computed* 'GO TO' that uses 'GO TO' and the 'SWITCH' declaration. The 'SWITCH' declaration is often considered to be a variable declaration since it appears in the variable declaration section of the program. In the following example, ONE, TWO, THREE, and FOUR are statement labels.

'SWITCH' X := ONE, TWO, THREE, FOUR;

Later in the program, this statement might appear as:

'GO TO' X(/I/);

The effect of the two statements is this:

When X has the value of 1, the 'GO TO' statement will shift program control to the statement labeled ONE. When X has the value of 2, control goes to the statement labeled TWO, and so forth.

While we've used the labels ONE, TWO, etc., in this example, for the sake of clarity, the statement labels following 'SWITCH' can be any allowable variable names.

Procedures

ALGOL is a *block structured* language. Each block starts with 'BEGIN' and terminates with 'END'. Each complete program is a block; it's also possible to have other blocks nested within the main program. These blocks may be assigned names and are known as *procedures*. Procedures are declared in the following manner:

'PROCEDURE' SUMVALUES;

This statement sets up a procedure named SUMVALUES. Procedures can make use of variables that are declared at the start of the main program. Also, additional variables used only in the particular procedure (*local* variables) may be declared in the usual manner after 'PROCEDURE' and before 'BEGIN'.

Ordinarily, constants, variables, and expressions used in the main body of the program are substituted by name instead of by value in the procedures. This means that the value of a variable is recomputed each time that it is needed in a procedure. To eliminate these recomputations, a constant, variable, or expression may be substituted in a procedure by value, instead of by name. This is done by 'VALUE' followed by the name of the variable, constant, or expression:

'VALUE' expression;

'VALUE' statements come between the 'PROCEDURE' identification and 'BEGIN'.

Input and Output Procedures

In its original form, the ALGOL language includes no input and output features; input and output functions must be handled through procedures. In 1964, a working group developed a set of standard primitive procedures for the input and output functions that have been widely adopted. Many ALGOL compilers include these procedures; they can be used as if they were statements on most systems.

A common output procedure is 'OUTREAL' which is used to output real variables. The general form of this is:

'OUTREAL' (output device, real variable);

The output device is symbolized by an integer. The real variable is output in floating-point form occupying 15 characters of space, including the positive or negative sign. Similarly, real values can be read into a system with the 'INREAL' statement, which has the form:

'INREAL' (input device, real variable name);

where, the input device is represented by an integer and the real variable will follow all the normal rules for variable names. This procedure will cause input data to be read until a sequence of characters forming a real value is found.

Similar procedures, such as 'ININTEGER', 'OUTINTEGER', 'OUTARRAY', etc., are available on most ALGOL systems for the input and output of integers and arrays. The procedure named 'OUTSTRING' allows for the outputting of literals and blank spaces.

Standard Functions

Some ALGOL systems also provide procedures for the following standard functions:

'*ABS*'—gives the absolute value of an expression.
'*ARCTAN*'—gives the arc tangent of a value.
'*COS*'—gives the cosine of a value.
'*EXP*'—gives the exponential function of a value.
'*LN*'—gives the natural logarithm of a value.
'*SIGN*'—gives the sign (positive or negative) of a value.
'*SIN*'—gives the sine of a value.
'*SQRT*'—gives the square root of a value.

Reserved Words

General practice calls for avoiding the use of any variable or procedure names that are (or begin with) any declaration, conditional or unconditional expression (or parts of one), standard procedures (such as 'ABS'), or 'BEGIN' and 'END'.

chapter 2

BASIC

Introduction

BASIC is currently the most widely used language for personal computer systems. BASIC (*B*eginners' *A*ll-purpose *S*ymbolic *I*nstruction *C*ode) was developed at Dartmouth College by Dr. John Kemeny and Dr. Thomas Kurtz as a teaching language. Elements of both the FORTRAN and ALGOL languages were incorporated into BASIC. However, the initial impression of BASIC is that it owes more to FORTRAN than to ALGOL, particularly due to the necessity for using line numbers. And, like FORTRAN, program control can (and usually does) shift back and forth abruptly within the program. BASIC assumes all variables are real unless otherwise declared. Output is simplified through the use of PRINT statements.

One unfortunate sidelight of the popularity of BASIC language has been the development of several different versions of BASIC for use with various personal computer systems. An entire book has been written dealing with just the different versions of BASIC language. In this book, only the most commonly used keywords and syntax will be discussed. For individual variations, the reference manual for the particular personal computer system being used should be consulted.

Program Format

Each line in a BASIC program requires a line number, as in the following example:

```
1000 PRINT "EACH LINE MUST BE NUMBERED"
9999 END
```

Line numbers can be any positive number between 0 and 65535 (0 and 32767 on some computers). Good programming practice calls for using line numbers in multiples of ten (10, 20, 30, 40, etc.) so additional statements can be added or removed as needed.

Remarks may be inserted into a program with the REM statement. The REM statement is nonexecutable; it has no effect whatsoever on the program. Its sole purpose is to document the program for other users and for future reference. The general form of a REM statement is:

```
1000 REM THIS IS A PROGRAM TO COMPUTE ACCOUNTS
```

Program execution starts with a RUN statement. If a line number follows RUN, execution starts at that line number. If no line number is included, program execution starts at the lowest numbered line. Program execution follows the numerical sequence of the statement line numbers until a STOP or END statement is encountered.

Variables may be introduced in a BASIC program as needed. There is no need to declare them before using them. PRINT and OUTPUT statements may likewise be included wherever needed in the program.

Variables and Constants

Constants are generally not recognized as being distinct in the BASIC language. A constant is simply a variable whose value does not change during execution of the program.

Variables are generally significant to only two places in BASIC. Also, all versions of BASIC allow the use of a single letter as a variable. Some versions of BASIC allow a letter and a number to be used as a variable as in Z2, J6, Y9, etc. Other versions allow variables to use up to 255 characters, although only the first two characters are recognized for distinguishing variables. For example, the variables ALPHA and ALWAYS would be read the same in some versions of BASIC since only the AL would be recognized.

Another variable type is the *string*. Strings are variables that consist of a group of letters or characters. String variable names end with $ to distinguish them from ordinary numeric variables. Some examples are:

```
AP$ = "JUMP"        ZL$ = "STRING"        VR$ = "VARIABLE"
```

Some versions of BASIC allow integer variables. These can be used for storing integer values (whole numbers) in the range from −32768 through 32767. Integer variables are indicated by % following the variable, as in Z9%, T4%, E2%, etc.

Another feature of some versions of BASIC is the ability to use *single-precision* (to six significant figures) and *double-precision* (to sixteen significant figures) variables. Single-precision variables are indicated by ! following the variable name (F5!, etc.). Double-precision variables are indicated by # following the variable name, as in D2#, L8#, etc.

Most versions of BASIC allow the assignment of values to variables by simply using the = sign, as in the following examples:

```
AS$ = "SUM"        P9% = 145        K5! = 0.123456
```

However, some versions of BASIC require using a LET statement in order to assign values to variables. To help ensure compatibility with other versions of BASIC, good programming practice calls for the use of LET statements.

Values for variables may be numbers of the appropriate type or expressions which evaluate to a numerical value. The exception to this, of course, is string variables.

Operational Symbols

The BASIC language uses the following symbols for arithmetic operations:

+	Addition
−	Subtraction
*	Multiplication
/	Division
↑	Exponentiation

Most versions of BASIC also provide for the following relational operators:

<	Is less than
>	Is greater than
=	Is equal to
< >	Is not equal to
< =	Is less than or equal to
= >	Is greater than or equal to

Also, most BASIC languages allow for Boolean operators, as follows:

AND   Statement is true if both expressions are true.
OR   Statement is true if either expression is true.
NOT   Produces the complement of a statement.

It is also possible to "add" two strings together. This process is known as *concatenation*. Concatenation is accomplished by simply using a + , as in:

```
L$ = "JOIN" + "STRINGS"
```

The most commonly used forms of BASIC also provide for the manipulation of strings through operational symbols:

<	First string precedes alphabetically
>	First string follows alphabetically
=	Equals
< >	Does not equal
< =	Precedes or equals
> =	Follows or equals

Operations in the BASIC language are performed in the following order:

1. Exponentiation.
2. Negation.
3. Multiplication and division in left to right order.
4. Addition and subtraction in left to right order.
5. String operators in left to right order.
6. NOT
7. AND
8. OR

The order of operations may be overturned by using parentheses. Operations in parentheses are performed first, with sets of parentheses in left to right order when nested within each other.

Program Control

Program control statements are used to direct the flow of operations within a program. Many of these set up a repeating loop of some sort. One of the most common types is the FOR . . . NEXT statement. The general form of this loop is:

```
FOR index variable TO final index value
    Body of loop
NEXT
```

This loop will repeat for a fixed number of times beginning with the first value of the index variable and continuing until it reaches the final value of the index variable. The index variable is an integer.

A variation of the FOR . . . NEXT loop is the following:

```
FOR index variable TO final index variable value STEP value
```

This variation increases the index variable value in increments that are indicated by the value following STEP. Thus, in

```
FOR I = 1 TO 1000 STEP 5
```

the index variable will increase to 1000 in steps of 5 (1, 6, 11, etc.).

A conditional branch statement is IF . . . THEN. It follows the general form:

```
IF condition THEN consequence
```

The condition is typically a variable and its relation is to a value or expression $(A > 4, B = (C + D)$, etc.). The condition could be another branching statement, an input or output statement, an expression, STOP or END, etc.

One common consequence of IF . . . THEN is GOTO. GOTO causes an immediate shift of program control to the statement whose number follows GOTO. An interesting variation of GOTO is ON . . . GOTO, which takes the general form:

```
ON index variable GOTO statement line numbers
```

An ON . . . GOTO statement causes the program to branch to different lines depending on the value of the index variable. In the following example:

```
ON I GOTO 10, 20, 30, 40
```

the program will branch to line number 10 when $I = 1$. When $I = 2$, the program will branch to line number 20, and so on.

An ELSE statement is frequently used to shift the program control in the event that a certain condition is not met. In the following example,

```
IF X > 5 THEN GOTO 200 ELSE GOTO 300
```

a value of X equal to 6 would cause a shift to line 200 while a value of X equal to 4 would cause a shift to line 300.

Input and Output Statements

One of the simplest and most versatile output statements is LIST. As the name implies, LIST causes the entire program that is stored in the memory of the computer to be outputted to the output peripheral that is in use. This is a very useful command if you did not write the program being used and you wanted to know what was in the program.

The most commonly used output statement is PRINT. The general form of PRINT is

PRINT item list

where the item list may consist of variables, numbers, or literals enclosed in double quotes. If variables are in the item list, their numeric values will be outputted, not the letters or characters representing the variable. For example, if $X = 50$, then PRINT X would produce an output of 50, not X.

The PRINT statement can also be used to cause mathematical operations to be performed. For example, the line

PRINT 2 * (10/2)

would cause 10 to be outputted.

A variation of the PRINT statement is PRINT @ (pronounced "print at"). This follows the form:

PRINT @ location output list

This causes the output to be printed at a specific location on the video display or line printer. Each individual system will have its own guide to its video display or printer to allow using PRINT @ correctly.

Another variation is PRINT USING. It is used to specify formats of numeric and string values in order to create desired output effects. The general form of this is:

PRINT USING string variable; variable

The string variable in a PRINT USING statement is known as a *field specifier*. It controls the way the variable is printed out. Consider the following set of statements:

```
A1  =  256.76735490
A$  =  "###.## "
```

The statement PRINT USING A$; A1 would result in an output of:

256.77

Note that the variable A1 has been printed out to the number of places specified and has been automatically rounded up to the nearest two places. The symbol # is used to specify the position of digits in the field specifier. The decimal point can be placed as needed within the field specifier.

Other symbols used with PRINT USING are:

,   Automatically inserts commas every three digits from the right when inserted between the first symbol of field specifier and the decimal point.

**   Will cause all unused space to the left of the decimal point to be filled with asterisks when placed before the field specifier.

$$ Will cause $ to be printed before number when placed before the field specifier.

Other symbols preceding the field specifier are allowed in various versions of BASIC.

TAB is used frequently with PRINT. It moves the cursor of the video display or printer horizontally to a desired spot on a line of output.

INPUT is commonly used to enter data into a BASIC language system. The general form of the statement is:

INPUT list of variables

INPUT is used in the following manner:

INPUT A1, B$

The statement requires entering a numeric value followed by a string variable. In a similar manner, variables must be entered in the order that they appear following the INPUT statement. Values entered are assigned to their corresponding variables. An INPUT statement is often used in conjunction with PRINT statements and literals to prompt program users to use entire required data. Attempts to input incorrect data (such as a numeric value into a string variable) will result in an error.

Another data input statement is READ. READ is used in

conjunction with a DATA statement to assign values to specified variables. The general form of READ and DATA statements is:

```
READ variable list separated by commas
DATA data list separated by commas
```

DATA statements generally follow READ statements but may appear anywhere in the program. Data in a DATA statement must match up with variables in the corresponding READ statement. Otherwise, an error will result.

A RESTORE statement is sometimes used with READ statements. It causes the next READ statement to start over at the first item in the first DATA statement. This allows re-using the same DATA items as many times as needed within a program. The usual form for using RESTORE is:

```
RESTORE
READ variable list
DATA data item list
```

Arrays

An array in BASIC language is defined as a single variable name used to arrange and store several elements of data. The elements may be numbers or strings. Generally, arrays set up a variable name followed by an integer number from 0 through 255. The general form of an array name in NUM(1), NUM (2), NUM (3), etc. These array variables are known as *single-dimension variables*. Array variables such as A (1,2,3) and Z(1,2,3,4) are *multidimensional variables*.

Arrays may be established by using a FOR . . . TO statement in the following manner:

```
FOR index variable TO final index value
LET array variable (index variable) = final index value
NEXT index variable
```

This is a cumbersome method. A much more commonly used method is DIM, a statement that establishes space in memory for an array of the specified number of dimensions and elements. For example, the statement

```
DIM Z(4)
```

would establish the array Z(0), Z(1), Z(2), Z(3), and Z(4). Note that the array will begin at zero, not one.

It is also possible to establish a multidimensional array using DIM. The statement DIM A(3,4) establishes an array with the following elements:

A(0,0), A(1,0), A(2,0), A(3,0), A(0,1), A(1,1), A(2,1), A(3,1), A(0,2), A(1,2), A(2,2), A(3,2), A(0,3), A(1,3), A(2,3), A(3,3), A(0,4), A(1,4), A(2,4), A(3,4)

The DIM statement appears at the beginning of any program using an array. One frequent use of arrays is to store information in a tabular form.

The maximum number of dimensions that an array may take varies among the different versions of BASIC language. However, most versions allow for an array of up to 255 dimensions.

Subroutines

A subroutine is a relatively independent portion of a program. It need only be written in the program once and it can be used as often as necessary. The program "departs" for a subroutine and, then, program control "returns" to the main program when the execution of the subroutine is finished. Subroutines are composed of numbered BASIC statements just like the rest of the program and all of the other rules of BASIC apply.

Subroutines are invoked with the GOSUB statement as follows:

GOSUB line number

This statement causes program execution to branch out to the subroutine. After the subroutine is executed, program control is switched back to the main program by a RETURN statement. Program execution resumes at the next line following the GOSUB. Good programming practice calls for subroutine numbers to be different from those used in the main program. For example, if the main program used three-digit line numbers, the subroutines should use four-digit numbers.

A variation of the GOSUB statement is ON . . . GOSUB. This, like ON . . . GOTO, will shift the program control to different subroutines depending upon the value of an index variable. The general form of this statement is

ON index variable GOTO subroutine line numbers

25

STOP and END Statements

A STOP statement interrupts the execution of a program and prints the following message on the output device of the system:

BREAK IN line number

A STOP statement is frequently used to stop the execution of a program if an irregular or abnormal condition is encountered, such as a negative score in a series of test results.

An END statement terminates the program execution normally, without any BREAK IN message. Many versions of BASIC require an END as the last statement in a program; good practice calls for it to always be used as the last statement.

Direct Memory Access

Microprocessor-based systems allow the use of POKE and PEEK statements for direct access to memory locations. Memory locations in most systems using BASIC are one byte in size, meaning that they can hold a number from 0 to 255. Most microcomputers have a maximum of 16,000 to 32,000 such locations.

A number of 0 to 255 can be placed in a memory location using a POKE statement. The general form of this is:

POKE memory location, data to be stored

The memory location is a positive integer expression denoting the memory location where the data is to be stored. The data to be stored is a number or expression between 0 and 255.

It is also possible to read the contents of a specific memory location using the PEEK statement. The general form of a PEEK statement is:

variable name = PEEK (memory location to be read)

The effect of a PEEK statement is to read the contents of a specific memory location and assign the value stored there to the variable name.

PEEK and POKE statements have usefulness in controlling external devices and in graphic displays.

Specialized Input and Output Procedures

Some features have been added to the BASIC language as a result of the characteristics of the microcomputer systems that the language is often used on. One characteristic of microcomputer systems is the common practice of connecting peripherals to the central processing unit through various input and output ports. Since most microcomputer systems are based upon 8-bit microprocessors, port addresses fall into the range of 0 to 255. INP and OUT statements allow the program to directly access these ports.

The general form of an INP statement is:

INP (memory address)

which will cause the computer to read the output of the peripheral located at the specified memory address. An INP may be used with other BASIC statements, such as PRINT, to manipulate data outputted by a peripheral.

An OUT statement causes an effect opposite to an INP statement. It sends a bit of data to an output port through an address specified in the OUT statement. The data is then used by a peripheral connected to the output port. The usual form of an OUT statement is:

OUT port address, data outputted

where the port address is an integer between 0 and 255, and the data outputted is a value or expression that can evaluate to an integer between 0 and 255.

Many popular microcomputer systems use tape cassettes for mass storage. This has resulted in the creation of two commands for handling tape cassettes. The first is CLOAD. Its form is:

CLOAD program name

which causes the program following CLOAD to be read from the cassette tape and stored in the random-access memory of the microcomputer. The opposite of CLOAD is CSAVE, which causes a program to be entered onto a tape cassette. Its general form is simply:

CSAVE program name

Machine Language Subroutines

Higher level languages, such as BASIC, have some disadvantages when compared to the lower level (machine) languages that are used by the microprocessor chip itself. Machine language allows certain operations to be done faster than in BASIC and it also allows the performance of some functions that are difficult or impossible to do in BASIC.

BASIC allows subroutines that are written in machine language to be included within the body of a program. These machine language subroutines can be used by either a CALL or USR statement (which statement is used varies among different versions of BASIC). The general forms are:

CALL (address of machine language subroutine)
or
USR (address of machine language subroutine)

Program control will return to the BASIC program when a RETURN command is reached in the machine language subroutine.

VARPTR is frequently used in conjunction with machine language subroutines. It will give the memory address of a specified variable, allowing it to be readily used by the machine language subroutine. The general form of VARPTR is:

VARPTR (variable name)

Program Editing Commands

The BASIC language includes several features that are designed to simplify program editing and changes when used on systems that use crt terminals for input and output operations. These features vary among different versions of BASIC; only the most common are given here.

An AUTO statement generates line numbers automatically. If no numbers are given after AUTO, line numbering starts at 10 and proceeds in increments of 10. If one number follows AUTO, line numbering starts at that number and proceeds in increments of 10. For example, AUTO 5 would result in line numbers 5, 15, 25, 35, etc., being assigned. It is also possible to specify the number at which the numbering is to start and the increments in which it will be done. For example, AUTO 100, 10 would result in line numbers 100, 110, 120, etc., being assigned.

A CLEAR statement sets the values of all variables, both numeric and string, to zero or "null." It is commonly used during program testing or debugging.

A CONT statement is used to resume the program execution of a program after an END or STOP statement is encountered in a program. On some versions of BASIC, this statement is known as CON.

A DELETE statement is used to remove specific lines from a program. The usual form is:

DELETE beginning line number-beginning line number

However, to delete just one line, use:

DELETE line number

There is also a way to delete all line numbers from the first line up to a specific line. Use:

DELETE -line number

The only difference between this and the previous command to delete one line is the addition of a hyphen just before the line number. Thus, one must be careful in using a DELETE statement to avoid accidentally eliminating several lines of the program. On some versions of BASIC, DELETE is called DEL.

An EDIT statement allows changing of a specific line in the program without affecting other lines. The general form is simply:

EDIT line number

A NEW statement removes all program lines from the memory of the computer and clears all variable values. NEW is used simply by entering it into the computer. On some systems, SCRATCH is used instead of NEW.

A RENUM statement allows renumbering of the line numbers in a program. This is handy when one needs to insert extra statements into a program, yet the existing line-numbering sequence does not leave enough room for the additional lines. The general form of RENUM is:

RENUM first line to be resequenced, first number of new sequence, increment

If the number of the first line to be resequenced is omitted, resequencing will start at 10. The increment is the numerical step by which each line number will increase (25, 50, 75, 100, etc.). On some systems, RENUM is simply REN.

Program Debugging Aids

BASIC language includes aids for tracing program errors and

problems. One is DSP, which will cause the value of a variable and the line number where it is executed to be printed out. Its form is:

DSP variable

A TRON statement activates a tracing function that allows the user to follow the flow of program execution. Each time program control shifts to a new line that line number is displayed on the system's output device. This is especially useful when a program contains numerous subroutines and conditional statements, and one needs to confirm that they are actually being executed. TROFF is the command that turns the TRON function off. On some systems, TRON is referred to as TRACE and TROFF is called NOTRACE.

Library Functions

The following is a list of the most common library functions found in the BASIC language. Different versions of BASIC may not incorporate all of these functions or they may have additional functions not listed here.

ABS—result is the absolute value of an expression.

ASC—gives the decimal ASCII value of a string variable.

ATN—gives the arc tangent of an expression.

CHR$—gives a single element string, which has an ASCII value that is given by an expression in the range 0 to 255 (this function is the inverse of ASC).

COS—gives the cosine of an expression in radians.

DEF FN—declares a user-defined function. Both numeric and string variables may be used.

EXP—gives value of natural number *e* raised to a specified power.

INT—gives integer portion of an expression using the largest whole number that is not greater than the expression.

LEFT$—moves characters from the left end of a string into another string.

LEN—gives the length of a string.

MID$—moves characters from the middle of one string into another.

POS—gives the current position of the video terminal's cursor.

RIGHT$—moves characters from the right side of a string into another string.

RND—gives a random number between 0 and 1.

SGN—gives the sign of an expression.

SIN—gives the sine of an expression.

SPACE$—gives a string of spaces, of a length specified by the expression following the function.

SQR—gives the square root of an expression.

STR$—converts a numeric expression to a string.

TAN—gives the tangent of an expression in radians.

VAL—gives the numerical value of a string.

Reserved Word List

Reserved words vary among the different versions of BASIC. As a general rule, any word that is used as a statement, command, function, or debugging aid will be on the reserved word list for that version of BASIC. The following words are on the reserved list for almost all versions:

AND	GOSUB	NOT	RETURN
AUTO	GOTO	ON	RUN
CLEAR	IF	OR	STOP
CONT	INPUT	OUT	TO
DATA	LET	POKE	TAB
DIM	LIST	PRINT	THEN
ELSE	NEW	READ	USR
END	NEXT	REM	WAIT
FOR			

chapter 3

COBOL

Introduction

COBOL is an acronym for *CO*mmon *B*usiness *O*riented *L*anguage. It was developed in 1960 under the auspices of the Conference on Data Systems Languages (CODASYL), an effort spearheaded by the Department of Defense to standardize computer languages used by the Department of Defense and its supply contractors. The use of COBOL language was boosted by the Department of Defense when its use was specified in many defense contracts. Since then, its use has spread through business and industry to the point where it may well be the most widely known and used computer language in the world.

The strength of COBOL lies in its abilities when used in file manipulation. Handling large volumes of data (such as financial or inventory records) is a natural for COBOL. COBOL was also designed to make programs as readable as possible for nonprogrammers; on this point, it may be the best computer language.

The following is excerpted from the 1965 CODASYL COBOL edition published by the U.S. Government Printing Office:

> Any organization interested in using the COBOL specifications as the basis for an instruction manual or for any other purpose is free to do so. However, all such organizations are requested to reproduce this section as part of the introduction to the document. Those using a short passage, as in a book review, are requested to mention

"COBOL" in acknowledgment of the source, but need not quote this entire section.

COBOL is an industry language and is not the property of any company or group of companies, or of any organization or group of organizations.

No warranty, expressed or implied, is made by any contributor or by the COBOL Committee as to the accuracy and functioning of the programming system and language. Moreover, no responsibility is assumed by any contributor, or by the committee, in connection herewith.

Procedures have been established for the maintenance of COBOL. Inquiries concerning the procedures for proposing changes should be directed to the Executive Committee of the Conference on Data Systems Languages.

The authors and copyright holders of the copyrighted material used herein

FLOW-MATIC (Trademark of Sperry Rand Corporation). Programming for the UNIVAC ® I and II. Data Automation Systems copyrighted 1958, 1959, by Sperry Rand Corporation; IBM Commercial Translator Form No. F28-8013, copyrighted 1959 by IBM; FACT, DSI 27A5260-2760, copyrighted 1960 by Minneapolis-Honeywell.

have specifically authorized the use of this material in whole or in part, in the COBOL specifications. Such authorization extends to the reproduction and use of COBOL specifications in programming manuals or similar publications.

Despite such intentions, COBOL is far from a standardized language today. Hardware manufacturers have developed COBOL compilers for their systems that have incorporated changes in the language. As a result, COBOL is far from a portable language. In this book, we will follow "standard" COBOL as contained in the CODASYL specifications in large measure. For variations, consult the system manual for which a particular program is written.

Program Format

COBOL programs are divided into four divisions: *identification, environment, data,* and *procedure.* Each division may be further split into sections.

The identification division, like the name implies, includes material to identify the program. It must include the program name, and it can include any other information such as the author's name, the system written for, the date written, and general remarks or warnings.

The environment division lists the input and output files that the program will use and assigns their internal name to an external name using SELECT/ASSIGN TO statements. Additional sections may appear under this division depending upon the computer system being used.

The data division gives additional information about the files specified in the environment division. The arrangement of records within files and the arrangement of data within records are described in this division. All variables are also declared here.

The procedure division is where the actual computation of the program is performed. All executable statements are found here, and execution proceeds until a STOP RUN statement is found.

Sections may be further subdivided into paragraphs. Each paragraph has a heading name composed of not more than 30 characters. Paragraphs are broken down into sentences of one or more COBOL statements. Each sentence must end with a period followed by a blank space.

The Environment Division

Under the environment division is an input-output section. In this section is a FILE-CONTROL paragraph. Here each file is named and other information pertaining to the files may be given. A typical environment division will look something like this:

```
ENVIRONMENT DIVISION.
INPUT-OUTPUT SECTION.
FILE CONTROL.
    SELECT INVENTORY ASSIGN 'SYSIN' UNIT-RECORD.
    SELECT PRICELIST ASSIGN 'SYSOUT' UNIT-RECORD.
```

Here INVENTORY and PRICELIST are file names. The normal computer input device is referred to as SYSIN while the normal output device is known as SYSOUT.

The Data Division

The data division has two important sections. The first is the file section, which contains file description (FD) entries. These are followed by a structure definition of the records. One mandatory statement following FD is LABEL RECORD. It is used to indicate whether there are any label records in the program. STANDARD means that labels for the file exist; OMITTED means no records exist for the file.

For each file description, there is a DATA RECORDS ARE statement. This usually follows the LABEL RECORD statement. The name of each record follows DATA RECORDS ARE and should be 30 characters or less. The FD is *one sentence* long and a period only comes at the end of the FD. Each file must have an FD.

Each DATA RECORDS clause must be followed by a *level one number* and the record name, as:

```
DATA RECORDS ARE INVENTORY.
01 INVENTORY.
```

Level one numbers are followed by *higher-level entries* that describe formats for various portions of the record INVENTORY. These descriptions are accomplished through PICTURE statements. Like the name implies, this statement shows the amount of space, the type of characters, and the location of any decimal point.

The following characters are used to compose PICTURE statements:

A: Letter or space.
B: Space.
P: Denotes location of a decimal point outside the data item.
S: Indicates a space for an operational sign. It is always the left-most character and can be used only once.
V: Denotes location of the decimal point.
X: Any character.
9: Number.

Picture characters may be "compressed" by enclosing the number of times a character is repeated in parentheses. For example, 9999V9999 could be written as 9(4)V9(4).

Data pictures are divided into five categories:

1. *Alphabetic*—only contains character A.
2. *Alphanumeric*—only contains characters A, X, or 9. It cannot be all A's or 9's.
3. *Numeric*—only contains S, V, or 9.
4. *Alphanumeric Edited*—only contains A, B, X, or 9.

5. *Numeric Edited*—only contains B, V, 9, *, + , \$, comma, or a period.

It is also possible for a data record to have data arranged in more than one form. Consider the following:

```
DATA RECORDS ARE INVENTORY.
01 INVENTORY.
   02 VALUE-LIST.
      03 ITEM-NAME PICTURE A(30).
      03 STOCK-NUMBER PICTURE A(3)9(6).
```

This means that INVENTORY has data stored in a form called VALUE-LIST. Bytes 1 through 30 have only alphabetic characters. This has been assigned the data name ITEM-NAME. The next three bytes have alphabetic characters and are followed by six bytes containing numeric characters. These nine bytes are assigned the data name STOCK-NUMBER.

It is also possible to refer to the same data with different names and pictures by using REDEFINES. In effect, it allows the same storage space to be described by different data descriptions. In the previous example, VALUE-LIST could be redefined as a new name known as ORDER-LIST by the following sentence:

```
02 ORDER-LIST REDEFINES VALUE-LIST.
```

Higher-level numbers such as 03, 04, etc., follow REDEFINES and contain pictures and other descriptive material.

Level indicators in COBOL are always two digits. For structures following DATA RECORDS ARE statements, level indicators from 01 to 49 are used.

Following the file section is the work-storage section, where structure and variable declarations that are not file records go. Variable names must be declared using a *level 77 description*. These use pictures like file records, as in the following entry:

```
77 PI PICTURE 9V9(4).
```

It is also possible to give each variable an initial value by using VALUE:

```
77 PI PICTURE 9V9(4) VALUE 3.1416.
```

More complex data structures may be declared in the working-storage section using pictures and level numbers in a manner similar to the data records that we have previously examined. The only restriction here is that more elaborate data structures *must* follow the level 77 descriptions.

Procedure Division

The procedure division is where the actual computation is done in a COBOL program. The arithmetic operators are similar to those used in other languages:

+	Addition
−	Subtraction
*	Multiplication
/	Division
**	Exponentiation

COBOL also includes the basic arithmetic statements ADD, SUBTRACT, MULTIPLY, and DIVIDE. These are added to BY, FROM, GIVING, INTO, and TO. Some typical examples are:

```
ADD 3 TO 4 GIVING 7.
MULTIPLY 3.4 BY NUM1 GIVING NEWPRODUCT.
DIVIDE DIV1 INTO DIV2 GIVING DIVANSWER.
```

COMPUTE is often used with the arithmetic operators, as in COMPUTE ITEM1/3. Execution is generally slower when using COMPUTE, however.

ROUNDED, as the term suggests, causes the result of an operation to be rounded to the nearest least-significant digit. ROUNDED must follow the appropriate data name.

COBOL also includes the following relational operators:

>	greater than
<	less than
=	equal to

NOT can be inserted in front of a relational operator to negate the meaning of it.

Program Control Statements

Within the procedure division are found statements that alter the flow of program execution. One such statement is the unconditional GO TO statement, as in the general form:

GO TO data name

However, this unconditional form may be modified by additional statements, such as:

GO TO data name DEPENDING ON data name or statement

It is also possible to modify a GO TO statement when it is executed by an ALTER statement. To use the ALTER statement, the GO TO statement must be the only statement in the paragraph. In the following,

```
CONTROL-PARAGRAPH.
    GO TO SEQUENCE-1.
```

the GO TO statement is the only one in CONTROL-PARAGRAPH. But the statement

ALTER CONTROL-PARAGRAPH TO PROCEED TO SEQUENCE-2

will cause the GO TO statement to become:

```
CONTROL-PARAGRAPH.
    GO TO SEQUENCE-2.
```

Another variation is the GO TO . . . DEPENDING ON . . . statement. Its general form is:

GO TO data names DEPENDING ON data name

For example, the statement

GO TO PARA1 PARA2 PARA3 PARA4 DEPENDING ON VARIABLE

will result in program control shifting to PARA1 if VARIABLE equals 1, PARA2 if VARIABLE equals 2, PARA3 if VARIABLE equals 3, and PARA4, if VARIABLE equals 4. If VARIABLE does not equal 1, 2, 3, or 4, the GO TO statement is not executed.

Another common program control statement is PERFORM. Its general form is simply:

PERFORM paragraph name

which causes the program control to shift to the paragraph named. A variation of this is:

PERFORM paragraph name THRU paragraph name

which results in the program control shifting to the portion of the program that is identified. The number of times a PERFORM statement is executed can be varied by TIMES, as in:

PERFORM paragraph name, number, or data name TIMES.

A PERFORM statement may also be used in more complex combinations, such as:

PERFORM para1 THRU para2 VARYING data name FROM data name BY data name UNTIL condition

where para1 and para2 are paragraph names.

COBOL also allows for conditional shifts of program control. One common form is:

IF condition THEN statement

A variation of this incorporates ELSE:

IF condition THEN statement ELSE statement

Data can be moved from one area of storage to another by using a MOVE statement. It has the general form:

MOVE data name TO data name

Character Strings

The COBOL language allows for operations on character strings through the EXAMINE statement and its various forms. The EXAMINE statement counts or replaces a character within a data item. The counting form is:

EXAMINE data name TALLYING ALL character

which will give the number of times the character appears within the character string being examined. An EXAMINE statement can also substitute one character for another within a character string using the following forms:

EXAMINE data name REPLACING ALL character BY character
EXAMINE data name REPLACING LEADING character BY character
EXAMINE data name REPLACING FIRST character BY character

In the first case, the EXAMINE statement will go through the character string and will replace the first character with the second wherever it occurs within the character string. The second statement will do the same to the leftmost character, while the third statement operates on the first such character found in the string. In more recent versions of COBOL, the EXAMINE statement has been replaced with INSPECT. It is used similarly to EXAMINE.

TRANSFORM can be used to replace a character in a string each time it occurs with another character. The general form is:

TRANSFORM data name FROM character TO character

More recent COBOL versions eliminate the TRANSFORM statement and incorporate its functions into INSPECT.

Read and Write Statements

READ and WRITE statements appear in the procedure division. Before they can be used, two files must be allocated for their use by OPEN statements:

OPEN INPUT file name
OPEN OUTPUT file name

The READ statement moves a data item from a file and makes it available for use by the program. The general form of a READ statement is:

READ file name AT END statement

The WRITE statement can take several forms, including:

WRITE data name
WRITE data name AFTER ADVANCING number LINES
WRITE data name BEFORE ADVANCING number LINES

The last two statements control where the data is printed on the output device of the computer system.

Another output statement is DISPLAY. This causes literals to appear in the output to dress up the appearance. For example, the statement DISPLAY "THE ANSWER IS" X. will cause the words THE ANSWER IS followed by the letter X to appear in the output. Some computer systems use single quotes instead of double quotes with the DISPLAY statement.

Reserved Word List

As can be seen, the COBOL language has a very large number of reserved words. This list contains the most commonly used reserved words—other versions of COBOL may have additional or different reserved words. Consult the system manual for the version of COBOL that is in question.

ACCEPT	CONTROLS	GENERATE
ACCESS	COPY	GIVING
ACTUAL	CORR	GO
ADD	CORRESPONDING	GREATER
ADDRESS	CURRENCY	GROUP
ADVANCING	DATA	HEADING
AFTER	DATE-COMPILED	HIGH-VALUE
ALL	DATE-WRITTEN	HIGH-VALUES
ALPHABETIC	DE	I-O
ALTER	DECIMAL-POINT	I-O-CONTROL
ALTERNATE	DECLARATIVES	IDENTIFICATION
AND	DEPENDING	IF
ARE	DESCENDING	IN
AREA	DETAIL	INDEX
AREAS	DISPLAY	INDEXED
ASCENDING	DIVIDE	INDICATE
ASSIGN	DIVISION	INITIATE
AT	DOWN	INPUT
AUTHOR	ELSE	INPUT-OUTPUT
BEFORE	END	INSPECT
BEGINNING	ENDING	INSTALLATION
BLANK	ENTER	INTO
BLOCK	ENVIRONMENT	INVALID
BY	EQUAL	IS
CF	ERROR	JUST
CH	EVERY	JUSTIFIED
CHARACTERS	EXAMINE	KEY
CLOCK-UNITS	EXIT	KEYS
CLOSE	FD	LABEL
COBOL	FILE	LAST
CODE	FILE-CONTROL	LEADING
COLUMN	FILE-LIMIT	LEFT
COMMA	FILE-LIMITS	LESS
COMP	FILLER	LIMIT
COMPUTATIONAL	FINAL	LIMITS
COMPUTE	FIRST	LINE
CONFIGURATION	FOOTING	LINE-COUNTER
CONTAINS	FOR	LINES
CONTROL	FROM	LOCK

LOW-VALUE
LOW-VALUES
MEMORY
MODE
MODULES
MOVE
MULTIPLE
MULTIPLY
NEGATIVE
NEXT
NOT
NOTE
NUMBER
NUMERIC
OBJECT-COMPUTER
OCCURS
OMITTED
OPEN
OPTIONAL
PAGE
PAGE-COUNTER
PERFORM
PIC
PICTURE
PLUS
POSITION
POSITIVE
PROCEDURE
PROCEED
PROCESSING
PROGRAM-ID
QUOTE

QUOTES
RANDOM
READ
RECORD
RECORDS
REDEFINES
REEL
RELEASE
REMARKS
RENAMES
REPLACING
REPORT
REPORTING
REPORTS
RERUN
RESERVE
RESET
RETURN
REVERSED
REWIND
RIGHT
ROUNDED
RUN
SAME
SEARCH
SECTION
SECURITY
SEEK
SELECT
SENTENCE
SEQUENTIAL
SET
SIGN
SIZE
SORT

SOURCE
SOURCE-COMPUTER
SPACE
SPACES
SPECIAL-NAMES
STANDARD
STATUS
SUBTRACT
SUM
SYNC
SYNCHRONIZED
TALLY
TALLYING
TAPE
TERMINATE
THAN
THROUGH
THRU
TIMES
TYPE
UNIT
UNTIL
UPON
USAGE
USE
USING
VALUE
VALUES
VARYING
WHEN
WITH
WORDS
WORKING-STORAGE
ZERO
ZEROES
ZEROS

chapter 4

FORTRAN

Introduction

The popularity of FORTRAN may only be exceeded by the COBOL language. The FORTRAN (*Formula Translator*) language was developed in the late 1950's by IBM and it was standardized in 1966 by the American National Standards Institute. While variations in the FORTRAN language do exist today, it is much more uniform than most other programming languages.

FORTRAN closely follows mathematical and algebraic notation in many respects. Not surprisingly, the "number crunching" ability of FORTRAN is quite powerful. Its mathematical orientation also makes the language relatively easy for most scientists and engineers to learn.

Early versions of FORTRAN were quite limited in their ability to edit output data into the desired forms, although later revisions have improved capabilities in this respect. FORTRAN also is more limited in its ability to process alphabetic data. Finally, FORTRAN programs often have several abrupt shifts in program control from one area of the program to another, increasing the likelihood of errors and often making a FORTRAN program difficult for others to understand. Balanced against these shortcomings are the still-impressive mathematical computation abilities of the language.

Program Format

Line numbers are frequently used in the FORTRAN language, although there is no requirement that each line be numbered. Line numbers as large as 99999 may be used. Unlike some other languages, there is no "begin" keyword to denote the start of a FORTRAN program. Each program must be terminated with END, however.

There is no requirement in FORTRAN for all variables to be declared in a single section or for all input/output statements to be grouped together. Variables may be introduced in the program as required and values can be assigned to them within the program or through data input into the program. Output can be made where desired. Subprograms that are completely independent programs in their own right must be placed after the main program, and before any data.

There is no punctuation placed at the end of a FORTRAN line. Commas can be used to separate items (variables, numbers, etc.) on the same line. Since FORTRAN was developed for use on keypunch systems, FORTRAN statements follow rules based on 80-character keypunch cards. Statements are written in spaces 7 through 72 of a program line. If a statement must be longer than this, it may be continued on the next line by inserting a character, other than zero, in the sixth space from the left side of the line on which the statement is continued. Good programming practice calls for using $ in the sixth space for statement continuations. Spaces 73 through 80 of each program line are unused.

Statement labels are placed in the first five spaces from the left of each line. Nonexecuted comments can be placed in a program by placing a C in the first space at the left of each line. Spacing between items in a statement is not important since the FORTRAN language ignores blank spaces.

Variables

The two most commonly used variable types in the FORTRAN language are integer and real. Variable names must begin with a letter and can be a combination of up to six letters or numbers; some versions of FORTRAN allow longer variable names to be used but only the first six characters are recognized for differentiating between variable names.

An integer variable can be established simply by beginning the variable name with the letters I, J, K, L, M, or N. Thus, MM, INT, INT22, and LENGTH are all integer variables. They can contain only integer values. Real variables can be established by beginning the variable name with a letter *other than* I, J, K, L, M, or N. Thus, TOTAL, SUM5, and P1981 are all real variables. Real variables can contain integer values as long as they are in real form; i.e., 12.0 instead of 12.

It is possible to "override" the restrictions outlined above by a *type declaration statement*. For example, DELTA would normally be the name of a real variable. However, it may be declared an integer by using the following statement:

INTEGER DELTA

In a similar fashion, a variable name that would ordinarily be an integer can be declared to be real.

Type declaration statements can be used to establish the following types of variables as well:

Complex—variables whose values are complex numbers.
Logical—variables whose values are true or false.
Double Precision—variables with 16 decimal digits.

Some systems also provide for variables whose values are octal and hexadecimal numbers.

The type of a variable must be declared before its use in the program or in a subprogram. This does not apply, of course, if one lets the system automatically assign variable types (I through N for integer, rest of the alphabet for real).

Values for variables may be assigned simply by use of the = symbol:

INTSUM = 45
TOTAL = 423.557

Values for variables may be assigned as the result of computation or because of input into the computer by READ and DATA statements (to be discussed later).

A constant is simply a variable whose value does not change. Constants follow the same general rules as variables.

Operational Symbols

The FORTRAN language uses the following symbols for arithmetic operations:

+   Addition
−   Subtraction

*	Multiplication
/	Division
**	Exponentiation

Operations are performed from left to right in the following order:

1. Exponentiation.
2. Multiplication and division.
3. Addition and subtraction.

The order may be altered by the use of parentheses. Operations in parentheses are performed first.

FORTRAN also includes several logical operators (sometimes referred to as relational operators). These are used to compare two expressions and give a result of true or false. Logical operators are:

.LT.	Less than
.LE.	Less than or equal to
.EQ.	Is equal to
.NE.	Not equal to
.GE.	Greater than or equal to
.GT.	Greater than
.NOT.	Negates
.AND.	Both
.OR.	Either

Unconditional Control Statements

Statements in a FORTRAN program are normally executed in the order in which they appear in a program. However, it is possible to interrupt the normal sequence by the use of control statements. Unconditional control statements alter the sequence of execution regardless of other factors in the program.

The most commonly used unconditional control statement is STOP. STOP causes execution of the program to terminate. A STOP statement is not the same as END; END is a nonexecutable statement that merely marks the end of the program for the compiler.

Another common unconditional control statement is GO TO (sometimes written GOTO). This statement causes program control to automatically shift to the statement number following GO TO. The statement

GO TO 99

will always result in program control shifting to the statement labeled 99.

Conditional Control Statements

The most common conditional control statement is IF. The general form for it is:

IF condition   consequence

A statement such as IF NSUM .EQ. 50 GO TO 99 would cause the program control to shift to statement number 99 whenever the variable NSUM equaled 50.

One variation of the general IF statement is known as the *arithmetic IF*. This will cause program control to shift depending upon the outcome of a mathematical operation. Its general form is:

IF mathematical operation   statement 1, statement 2, statement 3

When an arithmetic IF is executed, the mathematical operation is performed and a value is obtained. If the result is negative, program control shifts to statement 1. If the value is zero, program control shifts to statement 2. If the value is positive, program control shifts to statement 3. Statement numbers must be separated by commas.

Another variation is the *logical IF*. There are two general forms of logical IF statements. The first is:

IF relational expression   consequence

An example of this is

IF (NSUM**2 .LT. SUM*NSUM) PRD/A

The relational operation will be performed and a result (true or false) obtained. If the result is true, the operation following the relational operation is also performed. If the value is false, the second operation is not performed.

A second form of logical IF has the format:

IF relational expression   statement 1, statement 2

The relational expression gives a value of true or false when evaluated. If it is true, program control shifts to statement 1. If it is false, control shifts to statement 2. (This second form of the logical IF statement is not available on all FORTRAN systems.)

DO Loops

Another common conditional control construction is the *DO loop*. DO loops utilize a DO statement of the form:

DO statement label   index variable   first value, last value, increment

DO loops are terminated by a CONTINUE statement. Thus, a typical DO loop may look like this:

```
    DO 25    I = 1, 100, 2
    PRINT, NSUM
25 CONTINUE
```

The DO loop just discussed will cause the variable NSUM to be output on the printer or video terminal of the system. The loop will begin with the index variable at 1 and will continue until the index variable reaches a value of 100. The index variable will increase in increments of 2 each time the loop is performed, meaning that the loop will be performed a total of 50 times before the index variable reaches 100.

Any number of statements can be inserted between DO and CONTINUE. If the index variable is to increase in steps of 1, there is no need to include the increment. Thus, DO 50   K = 1, 25 will cause the loop to be executed in steps of 1 for a total of 25 times.

Extended Control Statements

Some versions of FORTRAN provide for additional conditional control statements involving DO loops. One is the IF/THEN/ELSE statement. It has the general form:

```
IF condition THEN DO
statements
ELSE DO
statements
END IF
```

In this case, the condition is evaluated by the computer. If the condition is met, the statements following THEN DO are executed. If the condition is not met, the statements following ELSE DO are executed. The END IF statement serves a function similar to CONTINUE in an ordinary DO loop, serving simply to terminate the loop.

The WHILE/DO statement allows for the executing of a loop as long as a specified condition is met. It has the general form:

```
WHILE  condition  DO
statements
END WHILE
```

with END WHILE serving to terminate the loop.

The DO CASE statement may be thought of as a multiple DO loop. It has the general form:

```
DO CASE index variable
first group of statements
CASE
second group of statements
CASE
third group of statements
.....
END CASE
```

The index variable can assume integer values such as 1, 2, 3, etc. If the value is 1, the first group of statements will be executed. If the value is 2, the second group of statements will be executed, and so forth, for all values that the index variable takes. If the index variable takes a value not covered by a CASE statement, then none of the statements in the DO CASE loop are executed. If desired, a group of statements may be included under an IF NONE DO statement that is placed after the last CASE statement and its group of statements. The statements following IF NONE DO will be executed if the index variable falls outside the range of values provided for in the DO CASE loop.

Arrays

Arrays of subscripted variables may be set up using the DIMENSION statement. It has the general form:

```
DIMENSION  variable (upper limit of array)
```

For example, the statement DIMENSION XSUM(10) would set up the variables XSUM(1), XSUM(2), XSUM(3), etc., until XSUM(10) was reached. It is also possible to establish arrays with more than one subscript; thus, DIMENSION XSUM(5,5,5) would set up an array beginning with XSUM(1,1,1) and continuing up to XSUM(5,5,5).

Subprograms

Subprograms are portions of a FORTRAN program that are defined separately from the main body of the program. The most common subprogram type is the *subroutine,* which is an independent program in its own right. The most common form of a subroutine is:

```
SUBROUTINE name (subroutine variables)
statements
RETURN
END
```

Any name that is a correct variable name can be used to name a subprogram. A RETURN sends the program control back to the point where the subroutine was "called" by the main program. An END marks the end of the subroutine, the same way it does in the main program.

The subroutine variables are "dummy" variable names used within the subroutine itself. The values of the subroutine variables are "transferred" to variables in the main program whenever the subroutine is used. Subroutines are used by employing the CALL statement. The general form of the CALL statement is:

```
CALL subroutine name (arguments)
```

The arguments in parentheses in the CALL statement may be variables or actual numbers. If the argument is a variable, the value of the variable is transferred to the subroutine variable. If the argument is a number, the subroutine value assumes the value of that number.

Suppose that a subroutine has been written to find the factorial of a number. It can be declared, along with a subroutine variable X, in the following manner:

```
SUBROUTINE FACTOR(X)
statements
RETURN
END
```

This gives the name FACTOR to the subroutine. In the main program, the factorial of 10 can be found by writing:

```
CALL FACTOR(10)
```

which causes the value of 10 to be transferred to X. Once the factorial of X is found, the value is "transferred" back to the main program.

As mentioned earlier, arguments can be variables as well. For example, suppose the variable INTSUM had the value 10. Thus, the statement CALL FACTOR(INTSUM) would have the same result as CALL FACTOR(10). In the former case, the value of INTSUM would be transferred to X within the subroutine and then "transferred back" once again to the main program after the subroutine had been performed. The result of using CALL FACTOR(INTSUM) and CALL FACTOR(10) would be the same—the factorial of 10.

A variation of the subroutine is the *function subprogram*. It gives a single value constant as a result, while a subroutine can give any number of different constants as a result. Both subroutines and function subprograms are placed at the end of the main program, before any data input.

Remote Block Units

Remote block units are like subroutines, except that they are not separate programs in their own right, and they do not "communicate" with the main program through arguments. A remote block unit follows the form:

```
REMOTE BLOCK name
statements
END BLOCK
```

where the name can be any valid variable name. A remote block can be established anywhere in the main program. It can be used simply by placing the name of the remote block after an EXECUTE statement.

Library Functions

FORTRAN language includes several library functions. Among the most common are:

ABS—result is the absolute value of an expression.

ACOS—result is the arc cosine of an expression.

AINT—result is a truncated real value.

ALOG—result is natural logarithm of X.

ALOG10—result is the common logarithm of X.

AMAX0—result gives the largest of two or more integer values in real form.

AMAX1—result is the largest of two or more real values.

AMIN0—result is the smallest of two or more integer values given in real form.

AMIN1—result is smallest of two or more real values.

AMOD—result is the remainder of a real number division.

ASIN—result is the arc sine of a real value.

ATAN—result is the arc tangent of a real value.

ATAN2—result gives the arc tangent of Y/X.

COS—result is the cosine of a real value.

COSH—result is the hyperbolic cosine of a real value.

EXP—result is the natural number *e* raised to specified power.

FLOAT—result is the real form of an integer value.

IABS—result is the absolute value of an integer.

ISIGN—this transfers sign of one integer value to another.

INT—this converts a real value to an integer value.

MAX0—result is the largest of two or more integer values.

MAX1—result is the largest of two or more real values converted to integer form.

MIN0—result is the smallest of two or more integer values.

MIN1—result is the smallest of two or more real values converted to integer form.

MOD—result is the remainder of an integer division.

SIGN—result transfers sign from one real value to another.

SIN—result is the sine of a real value.

SINH—result is the hyperbolic sine of a real value.

SQRT—result is the square root of a real value.

TAN—result is the tangent of a real value.

TANH—result is the hyperbolic tangent of a real value.

Storage Allocation

One method of allocating storage "space" for data is the ARRAY, and the DIMENSION statement mentioned earlier. Another method uses the COMMON statement. Normally, variables in the main program and in the subprograms are independent of each other. This means the variable name NSUM could be used to represent one value in the main program and an entirely different one in a subprogram. This also explains why arguments are often used to allow subprograms to "communicate" with the main program. The COMMON statement allows a variable name to have the same value in the main program and subprogram. The general form is:

COMMON first variable, second variable, etc.

which makes each named variable "share" common storage space for use in the main program and the subprograms.

The EQUIVALENCE statement allows two or more names to be used for the same variable. For example, the variable NSUM might have a value of 10. The statement EQUIVALENCE (NSUM, INT) would mean that INT would also have the value of 10. Further, if the value of NSUM were to change during the program, the value of INT would change as well.

The CHARACTER Declaration

Some versions of FORTRAN allow variables composed of various characters. These variables must be declared and the number of characters in each variable must be specified. This is done with a CHARACTER statement in the following manner:

CHARACTER variable name * number of characters

For example, CHARACTER TITLE*25 establishes a character variable named TITLE that contains 25 characters.

Input and Output Statements

The basic output statement in the FORTRAN language is WRITE. The general form of a WRITE statement is:

WRITE (output medium, statement label) variable(s)

The parentheses include two numbers. The first number specifies the medium to be used for the output. For example, 1 could be a video terminal, 2— a printer, 3— a disc storage device, etc. The second number is a statement label.

Another common output statement available on many FORTRAN systems (although not all) is PRINT. Its form is simply:

PRINT, first variable, second variable, etc.

A PRINT statement also allows the outputting of character data simply by enclosing it in single quotes. The statement PRINT, 'CHARACTER OUTPUT' would result in CHARACTER OUTPUT appearing on the output device.

The basic input statement is READ. Its form on most systems is simply:

READ, first variable, second variable, etc.

Each READ statement starts reading a new line of input and

continues reading until a value has been assigned to each variable following READ.

Values may also be assigned to variables by the DATA statement. The DATA statement is not executed when the program is run; it merely sets up a memory location for each variable name and value when the program is compiled. The general form of a DATA statement is:

DATA variable names /values/

For example, the statement DATA A, B /2.4, 3.78/ assigns A a value of 2.4, and B the value of 3.78.

Formatted Input and Output

Input and output in FORTRAN language is usually "formatted." This means that it is possible to specify exactly how the computer will read input data and the form in which data will be output. This is done with the FORMAT statement and *field descriptors*. The general form of the FORMAT statement is:

label   FORMAT(field descriptors)

FORMAT statements always follow input and output statements. A typical form of a statement might be as follows:

```
        WRITE (50) NSUM
50      FORMAT (I4)
```

When executed, the WRITE statement will cause the variable NSUM to be output in the form specified by statement 50. Statement 50 has a field descriptor of I4. This means that four spaces are to be used to output NSUM in an integer form. If NSUM has a value of 1234, all four spaces will be used. If NSUM has a value of 99, only two of the four spaces will be used. The output in such case will be *right-justified*, meaning that 99 will appear in the two spaces furthest to the right. The two "leftover" spaces to the left will be blank.

Sometimes a field descriptor may not be adequate for the desired output. Suppose, in the above example, that NSUM had the value of 55555, which occupies more than four spaces. In such a case, the space set aside for NSUM will be filled with asterisks, as in ****.

Field descriptors consist of a letter followed by a numeric indication of the number of spaces to be set aside for the variable. The field descriptors used for an output include:

I field—used for integer values.

F field—field used for real values. The usual form is (F total spaces.decimal places). An example is (F9.5), which means a total of nine spaces (including the decimal point) have been set aside for the real variable. The "5" means that five of the nine places will be to the right of the decimal point.

E field—similar in format to the F field, but the value is printed in exponential form.

G field—combines features of both F and E fields. If there is room, the value will be output in F form. If it is too large, output will be in E form.

A field—used for character data.

D field—used for double-precision values.

X field—used to insert blank spaces.

L field—used for logical (true or false) values.

H field—used for printing headings and introductory material (such as THE VALUE IS) along with values.

All of these field descriptors may be used for input except the H field. One advantage here is that a READ statement can "slice up" a stream of input data by using a FORMAT statement along with the READ statement. The input data that falls within various fields can then be assigned to various variable names.

Reserved Words

As a general rule, a keyword should never be used as a variable name. Good programming practice also calls for the practice of not using a keyword as any part of a variable name in order to avoid confusion.

chapter 5

LISP

Introduction

LISP is a relatively old language that has recently been the subject of renewed interest due to its suitability for artificial intelligence applications. LISP is an acronym for *LISt Processing* Language. It was developed in 1959 by John McCarthy at the Massachusetts Institute of Technology.

LISP is in many respects totally unlike any other commonly used programming language. It was primarily developed for nonnumeric computation, in direct contrast to other languages. It is also unique in its heavy emphasis upon recursive functions. LISP programs are a list of function definitions followed by the functions to be evaluated. Execution is not in the step-by-step manner of other languages, however. Each function definition is in the form of an expression. And, as might be expected from the term from which LISP gets its name, there is a heavy emphasis on list structures and notation.

Unfortunately, LISP has been developed in two main versions, EVALQUOTE-LISP and EVAL-LISP, and each system may not have all the functions normally given for its version of LISP. In addition, some functions may have somewhat different meanings on various systems. As such, it is impossible to cover here all the possible variations of LISP. In this chapter, we will restrict our discussion to EVALQUOTE-LISP unless otherwise stated. Also, some functions may have different definitions on some LISP systems than given here. One should always consult the LISP manual for the system being used.

Atoms and Lists

Atoms are the "words" of LISP. They are alphanumeric or numeric quantities such as ZARP, 530, DT43TT9, etc. Some LISP systems require that all atoms begin with a letter. Those are known as *alpha* atoms. Some LISP systems also allow for character strings. These are introduced by the symbols $$ and are "bracketed" by characters not appearing in the character string. For example, the character string CHAR could be bracketed by Y in the form $$YCHARY.

Lists are also "words" as far as the LISP language is concerned. Lists are built up from atoms and other lists. Lists follow the general format:

(any number of atoms and lists)

Some examples of lists are (EXAMPLE OF LIST), (WORD), and (LIST OF 1234). Lists may be joined together to form other lists by the proper placement of parentheses. For example, the "quantities" (THIS IS) and (A LIST) can be joined together to form the list (THIS IS (A LIST)). The placement of parentheses and the order in which lists are read follow the format:

(first list (second list (third list)))

and continue in the same pattern as additional lists are added.

One special list frequently found in LISP is the *null list*. It is simply ( ); it is also written as NIL. Most LISP systems consider NIL to be both an atom and a list. NIL is also used to terminate lists in some LISP systems.

Predicates

The LISP language includes a number of predicate functions that return either T (true) or NIL (false). The ones most commonly found on LISP systems are as follows:

EQ—This has two arguments. Its value is T if both arguments are equal. On most systems, EQ requires both arguments be atoms.

EQUAL—This is the same as EQ but it works with numbers and other arguments. It is "safer" to use this instead of EQ.

NULL—This is true if the value of the argument is NIL.

ATOM—This is true if the argument is an atom.

ZEROP—This is true if the value of the argument is zero.

Program Structure

A LISP program is in reality an extended expression. The expression consists of a function name followed by a list of arguments. Several such extended expressions may follow one another and the LISP will evaluate each one as it comes. The key point to understanding a LISP program is that most functions are defined recursively—they are inherently repetitive. The results of each repetition are usually dependent upon the results of previous repetitions. The ability to write or read a recursively written program is not easily picked up by many persons. Care must be taken when reading or writing LISP programs to observe the proper placement and matching of pairs of parentheses.

Basic Functions

The LISP language has several functions for the manipulation of lists. One is CAR, which gives the first element of a list. It is used as in:

CAR (THIS IS A LIST)

which gives THIS.

Another common function is QUOTE. When used with an argument, it gives the argument as a result. For example, the function

QUOTE (THIS IS A QUOTE)

gives THIS IS A QUOTE as a result.

CDR is a function that gives the remaining part of a list after deleting the first element of the list. The function:

CDR (THIS IS A LIST)

gives IS A LIST as a result.

CONS is a function that joins short arguments into a single longer one. The function

CONS THIS IS (A LIST)

gives (THIS IS A LIST) as a result.

Some systems also allow for the function LAST. This returns the last element of a list. For example,

LAST (THIS IS A LIST)

gives LIST as a result.

APPEND is a function that is available on some systems which joins two or more lists. The function

APPEND (THIS IS) (A LIST)

gives the result (THIS IS A LIST).

Some systems have REVERSE available as a function. As the name implies, REVERSE gives the elements of the list in the opposite order from which they are in the list. The function

REVERSE (THIS IS A LIST)

gives (LIST A IS THIS) as a result.

User Defined Functions

LISP permits users to define functions without naming them. These functions are known as LAMBDA functions. Their general form is:

(LAMBDA (elements) (expression))

The elements are usually atoms while the expression is an extended list as defined earlier.

Good programming practice calls for naming any new functions defined by the use of the DEFINE function. DEFINE is essentially a variation of the LAMBDA function in the form:

(Function name (LAMBDA (arguments) extended expression))

Once new functions are defined, they are added to the system and may be used like functions supplied in LISP.

PROG

LISP also allows for a more elaborate function known as PROG. PROG is short for "PROGram," and it simplifies the writing of certain types of programs. The PROG function allows for loops, assignment statements, and "go to" types of program control shifts. The evaluation of a PROG statement closely follows the rules by which statements are evaluated in ALGOL. GO TO statements are used with atoms serving as statement labels. The general form of a PROG function is:

```
(PROG (PROG variables) (arguments))
```

PROG variables are different alpha atoms. These are local variables used only within the PROG function.

Numeric Functions

While the LISP language is primarily of interest for nonnumeric computation, it has functions for numeric computation. Most LISP systems have the following:

ABSVAL—gives the absolute value of an expression.
ADD1—adds one to the value of an expression.
ENTIER—gives the integer part of an expression.
EXPT—one argument is raised to the power of a second argument.
DIFFERENCE—subtracts the following of one argument from another.
FLOAT—gives full decimal representation of an argument.
MAX—gives the largest of a group of arguments.
MIN—gives the smallest of a group of arguments.
PLUS—adds values of arguments together.
QUOTIENT—divides the values of two arguments.
RECIP—gives the reciprocal of an argument.
REMAINDER—gives the remainder after dividing two arguments.
SQRT—gives the square root of an argument.
SUB1—subtracts one from an argument.
TIMES—multiplies arguments together.

Set Functions

LISP also includes several features for the manipulation of sets. The following functions are available on most LISP systems:

INTERSECTION—gives a list of all elements that two sets have in common.
MEMQ—function giving T or NIL if an element is a member of a set.
UNION—gives a list consisting of all elements appearing in two sets.

MAP Functions

Many LISP systems provide for a group of functions known as the MAP functions. They allow writing short programs that perform complex operations. Most MAP functions are used only when all parts of a list are to be considered. The general form of a MAP function is:

```
(MAP function (LAMDA (list value)    ))
```

The MAP function will go through each expression of the list and apply a function to the value of each. The result of a MAP function is a list of values to which the function has been applied. MAP functions go by such names as MAPCAR and MAPLIST, where such functions as CAR and LIST are applied to all elements of a list.

READ and PRINT Functions

The LISP language has READ and PRINT functions. The READ function simply inputs an expression from the input medium. The PRINT function causes an expression to be printed on a new output line. On some systems, the PRINT function will return the value of NIL when used. Some systems also have PRIN1, which causes an expression to be printed out but which does not cause printing on a new line for each expression in the output.

Conditional Expressions

Most versions of LISP allow for conditional expressions through the use of the COND function. The general form of COND is:

```
COND (1  2)
     (3  4)
     (5  6)
```

A COND function is evaluated in the following manner. Argument 1 is evaluated. If it is not NIL, the second argument is evaluated and used as the value of the COND function. If the first argument is NIL, then argument 3 is evaluated. The evaluation of COND proceeds in this manner for all expressions.

Various LISP systems will have features and functions not covered here. Before any attempt is made to interpret a LISP program, it is essential to consult the LISP manual provided for the system that the program was designed to run on.

chapter 6

PASCAL

Introduction

Pascal is a relatively new language that has achieved wide acceptance in a remarkably short time. It was first put into operation in 1970 by Dr. Niklaus Wirth of Zurich, Switzerland. It was developed from ALGOL and, thus, shares many similarities with that language. Unlike most of the names of computer languages, Pascal is not an acronym; its name is a tribute to the seventeenth century mathematician Blaise Pascal.

Like ALGOL, statements in the Pascal language are separated by semicolons instead of line numbers. It is also block structured like ALGOL—meaning that programs are composed in blocks beginning with BEGIN and terminating with END. Each block is, in effect, an independent program. Pascal programs flow logically from beginning to end without the abrupt shifts back and forth that characterize such languages as BASIC and FORTRAN.

The Pascal language goes beyond ALGOL in allowing the users to define and manipulate new types of data other than the standard integer, real, array, and string types. This is a powerful tool in the hands of a creative programmer.

Program Format

The general format for a Pascal program is:

```
(* comment giving program name or description *)
PROGRAM name (INPUT, OUTPUT);
    Definitions and declarations
BEGIN (* program name *)
    Body of program
END. (*program name*)
    Data
```

Comments may be inserted into the program by placing them inside of the symbols (* . . . *), as shown in the preceding program format. These comments have no effect on the execution of the program and are solely for the convenience and understanding of the programmer and other users. Standard programming practice calls for beginning each program with a comment giving the program name or a description of the program. The program name follows as a comment after BEGIN and END. Comments should also be used to indicate PROCEDUREs, FUNCTIONs, and any potentially confusing blocks of the program.

Each program begins with a heading in the following form:

PROGRAM name of program (INPUT, OUTPUT);

The program name may be selected from a group of names known as *identifiers*. Identifiers must begin with a letter followed by any combination of letters and digits. Identifiers must not contain operational symbols or spaces, nor can they be words on the Pascal reserved word list. It is also a good programming practice to keep all identifiers distinct from each other in regard to the first eight characters.

Spaces may be used as desired to separate words and symbols in the Pascal language; in fact, separate lines may be used to separate words and symbols. The semicolon (;) must be used to separate individual statements from each other.

The *external files* of the program follow the name of the program in the heading. The external files are contained within parentheses. Normally, each program will have INPUT and OUTPUT as external files. Other files may be established as required. Files other than INPUT and OUTPUT must be declared as variables in the main body of the program. INPUT and OUTPUT are "automatically" declared whenever used in the heading.

BEGIN and END are used to establish limits for each block of the program. Simple programs may have just one BEGIN/END while more complex programs may have several. The final END in the program is followed by a period (.).

Various types of definitions and declarations follow the heading. Variables are assigned identifiers here and are declared as to type (INTEGER, REAL, etc.). New types of variables that are different from the standard ones provided for in Pascal are established here. Data is input into the program at the end of the program, not in the body of the program.

Variables and Constants

Constants may be declared in Pascal by a CONST statement. An example would be:

```
CONST MILE = 5280
```

Identifiers for constants follow the rules for all identifiers in the Pascal language. CONST statements appear in the definitions and declarations section of the program first, before other statements such as VAR and TYPE.

Every variable that occurs in the Pascal language must be declared by a VAR statement. The VAR statement associates an identifier with each variable and defines its type, as in:

```
VAR MAX, MIN: REAL;
    AMT, RATE: INTEGER;
```

Once declared, a variable's type is permanent. Its actual value may change (as from 10 to 20) but not its type (as from integer to real). Each program block can generally have only one VAR statement. However, as many variables as needed can be declared with a single VAR statement.

The standard variable types in the Pascal language are:

INTEGER—Values that are elements of the set of whole numbers.
REAL—Values that are elements of the set of real numbers.
BOOLEAN—Values that have the logic values of true or false.
CHAR—Values that are strings of letters and digits.

One of the most powerful features of Pascal is the ability for users to define and use value types other than INTEGER, REAL, BOOLEAN, or CHAR. This can be done using a TYPE statement such as the following:

```
TYPE DAY (SUN, MON, TUES, WED, THUR, FRI, SAT);
```

Values of the new type will be constants of the new type. The TYPE statements define values of a particular type, not variables of the type. A VAR statement is required to declare variables and must follow the TYPE statements.

Assignment Statements

An *assignment statement* computes a value and assigns it to a variable. "Values" are initially assigned to values by inputting data in the order that corresponds to the order in which the variables are declared. Assignment statements can be used to assign new values to variables.

Assignment statements make use of the following operators:

+	Addition with real and integer numbers.
−	Subtraction and negation of real and negative numbers.
*	Multiplication of real and integer numbers.
/	Division with real number result; operands may be real or integer.
DIV	Division giving integer result; both operands must be integers.
MOD	For remainder of integer division.
: =	Generalized equivalence statement; similar to = in conventional algebra.

Assignment statements are executed in the order that they appear in the program from top to bottom and from left to right. Further rules concerning the order of operations are:

1. Expressions in parentheses, regardless of preceding and succeeding operators.
2. Negation.
3. Multiplication and division.
4. Addition and subtraction.
5. Sequences of operations of the same type are done from left to right.

Some examples of assignment statements include:

```
NUM1 := 12
NUM2 := (12*9)/2.57
```

Control Statements

The Pascal language incorporates several statement classes to control the execution of a program. One group controls the number of times an action is repeated. One of the most common statements is the UNTIL statement:

```
REPEAT
    action
UNTIL
    expression
```

A variation of this is the WHILE statement:

```
WHILE
    expression
DO
    action
```

A more elaborate control statement is the FOR statement. It allows an action to be repeated for an exact number of times. The form of the FOR statement is:

```
FOR variable identifier : = expression TO expression DO
            action
```

Expressions in the FOR statement are usually integers but may be more complex expressions. A variation of the FOR statement substitutes DOWNTO for TO. This allows the statement to move from a higher valued expression to a lower valued expression.

Conditional Statements

Another group of statements selects between the alternatives based upon different conditions. One common statement of this type is the IF/THEN statement. Its form is:

```
IF expression
    THEN statement
```

A variation of IF/THEN adds ELSE as follows:

```
IF expression
    THEN statement
    ELSE statement
```

The GOTO statement is sometimes used in conjunction with other conditional statements. This is the only statement in the Pascal language that makes use of a line number. It is shown as follows:

```
    IF expression THEN GOTO 100
100 expression or statement
```

Line numbers must be declared using a LABEL declaration. LABEL declarations must come before VAR and CONST declarations that follow the PROGRAM heading. The form of a LABEL declaration is:

```
LABEL 100
```

Good programming practice in the Pascal language calls for using the GOTO statement only when no alternative method of structuring the problem exists.

Another useful conditional statement is CASE. It allows the selection among several different alternatives based upon the integer value of an expression. The general form of a CASE statement is:

```
CASE expression OF
   1. statement
   2. statement
   3. statement
      . . .
   N. statement
END (* of CASE statement *)
```

Relational Operators

Relationships between expressions are expressed in Pascal through the following operational symbols:

=	Is equal to
< >	Is not equal to
>	Is greater than
> =	Is greater than or equal to
<	Is less than
< =	Is less than or equal to

Another group of relational operators is used only with BOOLEAN operands. The operators and their meanings are:

AND	Statement is true if both expressions are true.
OR	Statement is true if either expression is true.
NOT	Statement is true if the expression is *not* true.

Input and Output Methods

A READ statement is the Pascal statement to input data. Data is inputted in the following manner:

```
READ (NUM1, NUM2, NUM3);
   data
   7 9 14
```

Data comes after the program and the individual data bits are separated by at least one space. Data is assigned to variables in the order in which they are inputted. In the preceding example, NUM1 would have a value of 7, NUM2 would have a value of 9, and NUM3 would have a value of 14.

A READ statement will only input data until it reaches the end of a line. If data is on following lines, the READLN statement must be used. This causes the input control to shift to the next line when the end of the first line containing data is reached. READLN can also be used to only partially read a line of data. For example, if four variables are listed following READLN, only the first four bits of data will be inputted and all succeeding bits on the same line will be ignored.

A WRITE statement is used to output data in Pascal language. Literals can be included in the output by placing them inside of single quotes. If a single quote is needed in the literal, it can be included by using double quotes, which will appear as a single quote in the output. Referring to the data in our READ example, we could have:

```
WRITE ('NUM1' 'S VALUE IS', NUM1);
      NUM1'S VALUE IS   7
```

While similar to READLN, WRITELN causes a shift to another line. Whenever the output specified following WRITELN is output, the program control shifts to the next line. This feature allows creative touches to the output of a Pascal program.

Procedures and Functions

A set of actions may be invoked several times within a program as needed through the PROCEDURE statement. The PROCEDURE statement establishes an independent programming block with an identifier. The usual form of a PROCEDURE statement is as follows:

```
PROCEDURE identifier;
      definitions and declarations;
BEGIN
      body of program;
END;
```

Note that each PROCEDURE statement is, in effect, an independent program. Variables can be declared and defined within a procedure statement just as in the larger program. In fact, since PROCEDURE statements are independent programming blocks, identifiers used within a PROCEDURE can be used in another PROCEDURE statement or in the main program (although good programming practice avoids this).

PROCEDURE statements can be used within the main program merely by using its identifier as an ordinary statement in the main body of the program. Each PROCEDURE can be used as many times as necessary within the main program. Each PROCEDURE statement must be declared by listing the full body of the PROCEDURE immediately following the VAR declarations in the main program body.

Closely related to the PROCEDURE statement is the FUNCTION statement. PROCEDUREs are sets of actions while FUNCTIONs are sets of actions that calculate *a specific value*. FUNCTION statements follow the same general rules and format of PROCEDUREs except that they are declared using the keyword FUNCTION instead of the keyword PROCEDURE. Pascal has several library functions available that will be listed later.

Arrays

An array in Pascal language is a fixed number of data components of the same type that are equally accessible. The ARRAY statement is used to establish an array in the following manner:

ARRAY [index] OF type

The index is generally of the form [1 . .N] with N representing the upper limit of the array. Multidimensional arrays can be declared by using arrays of arrays as follows:

ARRAY [index] OF ARRAY [index] OF type

A type of structure sometimes used with ARRAY statements is PACKED. This reduces the space required in storage by the data structure. PACKED precedes ARRAY, as in:

PACKED ARRAY [index] OF type

PACKED can be used and will have no effect on the meaning of the program, except that PACKED structures cannot be used as actual variable parameters.

ARRAY statements of CHAR type variables use PACKED ARRAY statements. These are used for generating strings in the Pascal language.

Files

A file is a data structure composed of a sequence of components that are all of the same type. The number of components in the file is known as its *length*. Files are sequential; they can only be processed (examined or additional elements added) in order in which the elements are arranged. Files are defined by using the form:

```
TYPE
    or        identifier  FILE OF   type
VAR
```

Files composed of CHAR variables are called *textfiles*.

Files used for input and output are called *external files*. The most common example is the (INPUT, OUTPUT) following the PROGRAM header. Additional external files can be added following the PROGRAM header but they must be declared as a variable in the main program. Files can also be used for purposes other than input and output; these are called *internal files*.

Records

A record is a data structure composed of components that may be of different types. It is also a random-access structure and may be updated or modified as desired. The general form of a RECORD declaration is:

```
TYPE  identifier        RECORD
            fields
      END
```

Fields are components of a record.

One problem with records is that their components will be processed by a sequence of statements. It would be much shorter in such cases if separate variables had been declared and used. The WITH statement lets one access the components of a record as if they were simple variables. The general form of a WITH statement is:

```
WITH  variables  DO
        statements
```

Sets

A set is a group of expressions of the same type. Sets are defined in the following manner:

SET OF type

Sets are processed as a whole, since there is no operation to break up a set into its components. Generally, any variable type but REAL may be used. Sets are indicated by enclosing them in brackets instead of parentheses.

The operator IN is used with sets to indicate whether a value is a component of a given set. It is usually used in conjunction with conditional statements or other operators, such as:

IF variable IN [set] THEN statement

Library Functions

ABS—result is the absolute value of X.

ARCTAN—result (REAL) is the arc tangent in radians of X.

CHR—result (CHAR) is a character in the position in the collating sequence given by the argument.

COS—result (REAL) is the cosine of X expressed in radians.

EOF—result is true if the end of file or end of data is reached; otherwise, the result is false.

EOLN—result is true if the end of the line is reached while reading the line; otherwise, the result is reached.

EXP—result (REAL) is e raised to power X, where e is the logarithmic natural number.

LN—result (REAL) is the natural logarithm of X, X > 0.

ODD—result is true if X is odd; otherwise, it is false. X must be INTEGER.

ORD—result (INTEGER) is the ordinal number of an argument X in the set of values of which X is a member.

PRED—result is the predecessor value relative to the argument value.

RESET—initializes an input file to accept values.

REWRITE—initializes an output file to output data.

ROUND—result (INTEGER) is value of X rounded from a REAL value.

SIN—result (REAL) is sine of X expressed in radians.

SQR—result is square of X.

SQRT—result (REAL) is square root of X.
SUCC—result is successor value relative to the argument value.
TRUNC—result (INTEGER) is value obtained by truncating
fractional part of REAL X.

Reserved Word List

AND	END	NIL	SET
ARRAY	FILE	NOT	THEN
BEGIN	FOR	OF	TO
CASE	FUNCTION	OR	TYPE
CONST	GOTO	PACKED	UNTIL
DIV	IF	PROCEDURE	VAR
DO	IN	PROGRAM	WHILE
DOWNTO	LABEL	RECORD	WITH
ELSE	MOD	REPEAT	

chapter 7

PL/1

Introduction

PL/1 (*P*rogramming *L*anguage 1) made its debut in 1965 as an ambitious attempt to combine the best features of FORTRAN, COBOL, and ALGOL into a single language. The result was a language whose capabilities were matched only by its complexity.

The versatility of PL/1 is indeed impressive. Its facilities for scientific calculations rival FORTRAN, and its ability to manipulate nonnumeric data is far superior. Like COBOL, the PL/1 language uses many statements whose meanings are readily self-explanatory, enabling a PL/1 program to be understood with a minimum of trouble by those not familiar with the language. And, some of the more interesting features of ALGOL have been included, although the total capabilities of the PL/1 language are vastly superior to any version of the ALGOL language.

Shortly after the introduction of the PL/1 language, it was predicted by many that PL/1 would be the single most important programming language of the 1970s. However, PL/1 fell far short of matching the FORTRAN and COBOL languages in popularity and, by the end of the decade, was slipping behind such languages as Pascal and BASIC in total usage. Part of the reason for the failure of PL/1 to meet the expectations planned for it is the complexity of the language; most implementations of the PL/1 language include over 200 keywords. Only a small portion of the capabilities of PL/1 can be utilized in most programming applications—the language is simply "too big" for many purposes. Also, the PL/1 language was introduced after the FORTRAN and COBOL languages were firmly entrenched. Many COBOL and FORTRAN users had no pressing need for the additional facilities of PL/1 and did not switch to the new language.

PL/1 still remains an interesting and impressive language. The sheer size of the language prevents us from covering all of its features in this chapter; only the most common and useful features will be mentioned. More complete information should be obtained from a system manual or user report.

Program Format

Any PL/1 program—either the main program or a subroutine—is called a *procedure* and must begin with the word PROCEDURE. All procedures must have a label preceding them. The PROCEDURE statement for the main program takes the form of:

label: PROCEDURE OPTIONS (MAIN);

and terminates with the word END. Likewise, all subroutines have a label before PROCEDURE and terminate with END. Labels may consist of up to 31 characters, and the first character must be a letter of the alphabet. All labels must be separated from statements by a colon (:). Sometimes a "break" symbol _ will be used in labels, as in TIME_OF_DAY.

Semicolons (;) are used to separate the statements from each other. Two or more statements may be placed on the same line (although normal programming practice discourages this). Each statement *must* end with a semicolon.

Comments may be inserted into a program by placing them between the symbols /* and */, such as:

/*   comments   */

Comments may be inserted between statements or even between the separate terms of a statement.

Program execution normally flows from top to bottom, although this can be modified through the use of the various control transfer statements and labels.

Variables and the DECLARE Statement

Variable names in the PL/1 language may consist of up to 31 characters, the first of which must be a letter of the alphabet. The symbols $, @, and # may be included as part of a variable name.

Numbers are stored in various forms by the PL/1 compiler. One form is REAL FIXED BINARY. In this form of internal representation, the number 8 would be stored as 1000.B, with 1000 being the base 2 equivalent of the decimal 8, followed by a decimal point and the letter B to denote the quantity is binary. Similarly, a number such as .125 would be stored as .001B.

Another form of storage is REAL FLOAT DECIMAL. This form uses a mantissa, then the letter E and a number referring to a base of ten. Some examples of REAL FLOAT DECIMAL numbers are 6.2E2, 5.E0, −87.1E6, and 3.3E-5.

Variables beginning with the letters I through N are automatically stored as REAL FIXED BINARY, while variables beginning with the other letters of the alphabet are stored as REAL FLOAT DECIMAL. This assignment can be overridden by the DECLARE statement.

A DECLARE statement allows specifying the *attributes* of variables. For example, the variable name LATITUDE would normally have its value represented in the computer in REAL FIXED BINARY form. But it can be stored in REAL FLOAT DECIMAL form by using the following format:

DECLARE LATITUDE REAL FLOAT DECIMAL;

Another common form of internal representation is REAL FLOAT BINARY, which is similar to REAL FLOAT DECIMAL except that the number is "exponential binary." A typical form is 1101E2B, with the B again indicating binary.

Some versions of PL/1 also allow for a COMPLEX attribute which allows for internal representations of complex numbers. However, the CHARACTER attribute is more common. This allows the variable name to represent a string of up to 256 alphanumeric characters. It is established by the following typical statement:

DECLARE NAME CHARACTER (15);

which allows NAME to be the name of a character string of 15 characters. The attribute VARYING indicates that the length of the string varies. For example,

DECLARE NAME CHARACTER (15) VARYING;

indicates that NAME is the name of a string that can contain up to 15 characters.

Closely related to the CHARACTER attribute is the BIT declaration. This declares a variable name that is used to represent strings of the specified number of binary digits.

A variable name can be used to represent any label used in the program by using the attribute LABEL with DECLARE. It is used in the following manner:

```
DECLARE A12345 LABEL;
```

which establishes a label named A12345. Labels are used with loops.

Operational Symbols

The PL/1 language uses the following operational symbols:

+	Addition
−	Subtraction
*	Multiplication
/	Division
**	Exponentiation
=	Equals
¬ =	Not equals
<	Less than
< =	Less or equal to
>	Greater than
> =	Greater or equal to
&	AND
|	OR
¬	NOT
||	Concatenation

The normal sequence of operation is for exponentiation to be performed first, followed by multiplication and division. Next comes addition and subtraction, then concatenation, relational operations and, finally, AND/OR operations. The ¬ symbol can be used to negate any relational expression. Operations are normally performed from left to right, with the exception of operations contained in parentheses which are always performed first. The concatenation symbol is only used with operations involving strings, whether bit or character.

The INITIAL Specification

When used with a DECLARE statement, INITIAL allows the

setting (initializing) of the values of variables. For example, the statement

DECLARE SUM FIXED INITIAL (500);

would cause the value 500 to be stored in SUM in REAL FIXED DECIMAL form.

Arrays

An array may be set up using a DECLARE statement. The general form used is:

DECLARE variable name (lower limit: upper limit) attributes;

Thus, the statement DECLARE SUM (1:10) would set up an array of SUM1, SUM2, etc., through SUM10. Additional dimensions can be specified by separating the index ranges by a comma, as in:

DECLARE SUM (1:10, 1:5) REAL FLOAT DECIMAL;

which will set up an array of SUM having index ranges for its two dimensions of 1 through 10 and 1 through 5. Index ranges can be declared in terms of arithmetic expressions which are evaluated to define the index ranges.

Names of arrays may be included in arithmetic operations without indices. In such cases, the arithmetic operation will be performed for each value for the index range. Sometimes, the first index value will be omitted when establishing a variable. In such cases, the lower index value will be assumed to be 1.

Sometimes the asterisk (*) will be used to denote the entire range of an index. Suppose an array has been established for SUM with the ranges 1 to 5 and 1 to 3. Thus, SUM (2, *) will denote the array SUM(1,1), SUM (1,2), and SUM (1,3). This is sometimes referred to as *cross-sectioning* an array.

Control Statements

The PL/1 language includes several statements used to alter normal execution flow of a program. One of the simplest, GO TO, transfers execution to a labeled portion of the program. Its form is simply:

GO TO statement label;

and causes control to automatically shift to the point indicated.

A conditional statement is the IF/THEN statement. Its form is:

```
IF condition THEN consequence;
```

which will cause the execution of the consequence depending on whether or not the condition is met. An alternative form is the IF/THEN/ELSE statement:

```
IF condition THEN first consequence ELSE second consequence;
```

which will cause the execution of the first consequence if the condition is met or the execution of the second consequence if the condition is not met.

Loops can be set up through the use of DO/END statements, as in:

```
DO;
Statements
END;
```

This will cause the loop to be executed once. Multiple executions can be set up by adding TO:

```
DO beginning index TO ending index;
Statements
END;
```

which will cause the loop to be performed once for each index value. Normally, the index count will advance by 1 each time the loop is performed. If a different advance is wanted, BY can be added after the ending index and the desired advance specified after BY. There is no requirement in the PL/1 language for the beginning and ending index values or advance increments to be positive integers.

A WHILE notation can be used to cause the execution of a loop as long as a condition is met. The general form is:

```
DO beginning index TO ending index BY increment WHILE conditon;
Statements
END;
```

An alternative form of conditional loop execution involves a variation of the IF/THEN loop. This is shown by the form:

```
IF condition THEN DO;
Statements
END;
```

An IF/THEN/ELSE statement can also be modified for use with loops in the following manner:

```
IF condition THEN DO;
First set of statements
END;
ELSE DO;
Second set of statements;
END;
```

Procedures

As mentioned earlier, PL/1 programs are made up of procedures. The main program itself is called the *main* procedure and begins with a program name followed by PROCEDURE OPTIONS (MAIN) as mentioned before. Other procedures may be included in the PL/1 program as needed. Procedures are identified by a name and they follow the form:

```
name: PROCEDURE;
Statements
END;
```

When a procedure is to be used, the statement:

```
CALL procedure name;
```

is used. When END is found in the procedure, it returns to the main program of the statement immediately following CALL. A RETURN statement within the procedure itself (for example, as a consequence of a conditional statement) will cause the same result.

If procedures in a program are arranged so that all the executable statements are located between PROCEDURE and END, the procedures are *external* to each other. Variable names and DECLARE statements are used only within each procedure. However, certain parameters (variable names, values, etc.) may be "transmitted" to and from a procedure by placing them in parentheses following the CALL statement.

A *BEGIN block* is similar to a procedure. It follows the form:

```
BEGIN;
Statements
END;
```

A BEGIN block is not executed by a CALL statement but, instead, is executed in the normal sequence of the program. However, all DECLARE statements in a BEGIN block are used only within the block, much like a procedure.

Procedures may call themselves either directly or by calling another procedure that uses it. These are known as *recursive* procedures. They can be established in the following manner:

name: PROCEDURE RECURSIVE;

Recursive procedures frequently are used to avoid the necessity for multiple DO loops.

The PICTURE Specification

A PICTURE specification is used to describe a character string. Each position within the string can be restricted to a single type of character, such as a letter of the alphabet, a numeral, a blank, etc. The following characters are used to make up a PICTURE specification:

X	Any character
A	A through Z, or a blank
B	Blank
V	Position of a suppressed decimal point
V.	. (period or decimal point)
.V	. (period) or blank if preceding character was replaced by a blank
Z	Replaces leading zeroes with blanks
S	Indicates + or −
9	0 through 9
,	, (comma) or blank if preceding character was replaced by a blank
+	+ character (positive)
−	− character (negative)
$	$ character

For example, the PICTURE 'AAAA' specifies a character string such as NAME or HOME. The specification '99999' is for a string of numeric characters such as 27514 and 92514. A PICTURE such as 'XXXXX' could be used for any combination of five characters. Note that all PICTURE specifications are enclosed in single quotes.

PICTURE specifications are established using a DECLARE statement:

DECLARE SUM PICTURE 'XXXXXXXX';

The PICTURE specification means that numerical quantities can be stored and manipulated as character strings.

String Manipulation Statements

The PL/1 language has several features for handling character strings. One of the most commonly used is the concatenation operator, ‖. This symbol puts together two character strings into a single new one. Suppose A is the string NEW and B is the string STRING. The statement

```
C = A ‖ B
```

would result in C representing the string NEWSTRING.

PL/1 has several built-in functions for string operations. One is LENGTH. The LENGTH function gives a REAL FIXED BINARY value equal to the number of characters in a string. Its general form is:

```
variable name = LENGTH (name of string);
```

Another function is INDEX. The INDEX function examines two character strings to see if one string is a substring (is part of) of another string. If one string is not a substring of another, the INDEX function gives it a value of 0. If it is a substring, the INDEX function gives it a REAL FIXED BINARY value equal to the position in bytes where one string first appears as a substring of the other. The general form is:

```
INDEX (first string, second string);
```

The INDEX function tests to see if the second string is a substring of the first.

A SUBSTR function will produce a substring of a string. It has the general form:

```
SUBSTR (string name, beginning position, length);
```

The beginning position is an integer representing the number of characters from the beginning of the string that the substring starts. The length is an integer representing how many characters of the string the substring will cover from the beginning position. If the length is omitted, the substring will have all the characters from the beginning position to the end of the string.

The TRANSLATE function can replace characters in strings with other characters. Its general form is:

```
TRANSLATE (string 1, string 2, string 3);
```

Every time the first character of string 3 occurs in string 1, it is replaced by the first character in string 2. In the same way, each time the second character of string 3 occurs in string 1, it is replaced by the second character in string 2. This process continues for each character and occurrence. String 2 and string 3 must be of the same length.

Two other string functions are STRING and VERIFY. The STRING function combines elements of an array into a single character string, while the VERIFY function searches one character string for characters not in a second string.

Input and Output Statements

There are two general forms of input and output statements in the PL/1 language. If the data must be converted from one form into binary, it is termed *stream-oriented;* if the data is in binary form only, it is said to be *record-oriented.*

One very common stream-oriented input statement is GET EDIT. It causes data to be read and assigned to variable names according to specified parameters. The general form is:

```
GET EDIT (variables) (parameters);
```

Data may be output in a similar fashion by the PUT EDIT statement, which follows the same general format as the GET EDIT statement.

The parameters used for GET EDIT and PUT EDIT statements are as follows:

F(n)	Fixed point numbers, with n representing the total number of characters.
F(n, d)	Same as F(n), except that d represents the number of places to the right of the decimal point.
E(n)	Floating point numbers, with n representing the total number of characters.
E(n, d)	Same as E(n), except that d represents the number of places to the right of the decimal point.
A(n)	Character strings, with n representing the total number of characters.
B(n)	Bit strings, with n representing the length in bits.
X(n)	Results in n number of characters to be skipped on input, or n number of blanks to be inserted on output.

The GET LIST statement reads in a list of variable names separated by commas. If the variables are part of an array, the entire array will be read in if the subscripts are not indicated. The PUT LIST statement causes data items to be printed in a readable form without the use of format parameters.

Closely related to the preceding statements are GET DATA and PUT DATA statements. Variable names may be used in both statements, although array names can be used only in PUT DATA statements. Suppose that the input is A = 10. It can be input into the computer using the statement GET DATA(A). On the output, the statement PUT DATA(A) would result in the output:

```
A = 10
```

A READ statement is used for the input of record-oriented data with a WRITE statement being used for the output of the same type of data. Most commonly, they are used with input and output files, which are set up by a DECLARE statement and a FILE specification. A typical declaration would be

```
DECLARE DISC1 FILE RECORD INPUT
```

which would establish DISC1 as a record-oriented data file used only for input to memory. An output file could be established just as easily by substituting OUTPUT for INPUT in the DECLARE statement. Files may be used for both input and output by using OPEN and CLOSE statements. Once a file has been declared to be INPUT and OUTPUT, OPEN and CLOSE statements can "reset" the file so that it can be used for the opposite function.

The PL/1 language allows a wide variety of data structures and files, much like the COBOL language. However, due to their complexity (and the difficulty in duplicating them in other languages), we will not discuss them here. A PL/1 system manual or user report should be consulted for more detailed information.

Reserved Words

There are no reserved words in the PL/1 language. Good programming practice calls for not using any keywords as the names of variables, files, etc.

chapter 8

Keyword Dictionary

The language that each keyword is extracted from is given after each definition.

ABS—Library function giving the absolute value of X *(BASIC)*.

ABS—Library function giving the absolute value of a real number *(FORTRAN)*.

ABS—Library function giving the absolute value of X *(Pascal)*.

ABSVAL—Function giving the absolute value of an argument *(LISP)*.

ACCEPT—Used in conjunction with FROM to input small quantities of data *(COBOL)*.

ACCESS—Clause specifying MODE by which records are accessed in a file *(COBOL)*.

ACOS—Library function giving the arc cosine of X *(FORTRAN)*.

ADD—Verb adding two or more data items *(COBOL)*.

ADD1—Function adding one to the value of an argument *(LISP)*.

AINT—Library function truncating a real value to lowest whole number *(FORTRAN)*.

ALOG—Library function giving the natural logarithm of X *(FORTRAN)*.

ALOG10—Library function giving the common logarithm of X *(FORTRAN)*.

ALTER—Verb used to change the point in a program where GO TO shifts control to *(COBOL)*.

AMAX0—Library function giving the largest of two or more integer values, result is given in real form *(FORTRAN)*.

AMAX1—Library function giving largest of two or more real values *(FORTRAN)*.

AMIN0—Library function giving the minimum of two or more integer values, result is given in real form *(FORTRAN)*.

AMIN1—Library function giving the smallest of two or more real values *(FORTRAN)*.

AMOD—Library function giving the remainder for a real number division *(FORTRAN)*.

AND—Logical operator indicating an expression is true if both expressions in the expression are true *(BASIC)*.

AND—Logical operator combining two elements into an expression that is true if both elements are true *(COBOL)*.

AND—Boolean operator indicating that an expression is true if both elements are true *(Pascal)*.

APPEND—Function returning a list composed of all the objects in two lists *(LISP)*.

ARCTAN—Library function giving the arc tangent in radians of X *(Pascal)*.

ARRAY—Declaration establishing an array of variables of a certain type *(ALGOL)*.

ARRAY (OF)—Definition specifying a structure consisting of a fixed number of components *(Pascal)*.

ASC—String function giving the decimal ASCII value of a designated string variable *(BASIC)*.

ASIN—Library function giving the arc sine of X *(FORTRAN)*.

ASSIGN (TO)—Statement that is used to assign an integer constant representing a statement number to a simple integer variable *(FORTRAN)*.

ATAN—Library function giving the arc tangent of X *(FORTRAN)*.

ATAN2—Library function giving the arc tangent of Y divided by X *(FORTRAN)*.

ATN—Library function giving the arc tangent of X *(BASIC)*.

ATOM—Function returning T if argument is an atom or NIL if it is not *(LISP)*.

ATOMLENGTH—Function returning a value equal to the number of atoms in a list *(LISP)*.

AUTHOR—Paragraph in identification division giving name of programmer(s) *(COBOL)*.

AUTO—Command starting automatic line numbering at a certain number and increasing by a fixed increment *(BASIC)*.

BACKSPACE—Statement moving a tape or disk back to the beginning of the previous file *(FORTRAN)*.

BEGIN—Statement starting a sequence of statements *(ALGOL)*.

BEGIN—Used in conjunction with END to denote the limits of a compound statement or an entire program *(Pascal)*.

BEGIN—Statement beginning a series of statements that are executed together in normal program sequence; it does not need a CALL statement to be executed nor does it need a label *(PL/1)*.

BINARY—Attribute indicating a variable is stored in exponential form using a base 2 number system *(PL/1)*.

BIT—Attribute indicating a variable is a bit string of a length equal to a specified number of binary digits *(PL/1)*.

BLOCK CONTAINS—Clause giving size of a specified file description *(COBOL)*.

BLOCK DATA—Heading for a subprogram containing only declaration statements *(FORTRAN)*.

BOOLEAN—Declaration denoting a variable having the values "true" and "false" *(ALGOL)*.

BOOLEAN—Type of variable whose value is either "true" or "false" *(Pascal)*.

BY—Indicates increments by which the index of a DO loop is increased *(PL/1)*.

CALL—Statement causing BASIC language program to branch to a machine language subroutine *(BASIC)*.

CALL—Verb used in conjunction with USING causing program control to program the portion that is named *(COBOL)*.

CALL—Statement causing execution of a subroutine depending upon the evaluation of arguments following the name of the subroutine *(FORTRAN)*.

CALL—Statement causing the execution of the procedure that is named *(PL/1)*.

CAR—Function giving the first element of a list *(LISP)*.

CASE—Used in conjunction with OF to indicate alternatives according to different values of an expression *(Pascal)*.

CDR—Function returning an argument less the first element *(LISP)*.

CHAR—Type of variable that is a set of characters *(Pascal)*.

CHARACTER—Statement declaring a variable to be a character variable *(FORTRAN)*.

CHARACTER—Attribute indicating the name of a string of characters *(PL/1)*.

CHR—Library function giving a result that is a character in the position in the collating sequence given by the argument *(Pascal)*.

CHR$—String function that gives a single element string which has an ASCII code that is given by an expression. The value of the expression must be in the range of 0 to 255 *(BASIC)*.

CLEAR—Command setting all program variables to zero *(BASIC)*.

CLOAD—Command loading a program from a cassette *(BASIC)*.

CLOSE—Verb ending file processing *(COBOL)*.

CLOSE—Statement which specifies that a file is not set to input or output data *(PL/1)*.

CODE—Statement specifying a literal that identifies print lines as being part of a specific report *(COBOL)*.

COMMENT—Declaration that the material that follows is a nonexecuted remark *(ALGOL)*.

COMMON—Statement specifying that a group of variables is to be kept in an area of common storage *(FORTRAN)*.

COMPLEX—Statement declaring a variable to have a complex value *(FORTRAN)*.

COMPLEX—Attribute indicating a variable is a complex number *(PL/1)*.

COMPUTATIONAL—Clause identifying a type of data USAGE for data items used in computations. They must be numeric and pictures for them can contain only 9, S, V, P, or parentheses *(COBOL)*.

COMPUTE—Verb evaluating an arithmetic expression and assigning it to a data item *(COBOL)*.

CON—Same as CONT in some versions of BASIC *(BASIC)*.

CONS—Function returning a single list from two separate lists *(LISP)*.

CONST—Declaration used to give names to quantities that do not change throughout a program *(Pascal)*.

CONT—Command continuing program execution after a STOP or END statement *(BASIC)*.

CONTINUE—Statement used to terminate a DO loop *(FORTRAN)*.

CONTROL—Clause creating levels of a control hierarchy for a report *(COBOL)*.

COPY—Verb inserting a library text into a program during compilation *(COBOL)*.

CORRESPONDING—Phrase used with ADD, SUBTRACT, or MOVE to allow corresponding data items from two groups to be used as operands in arithmetic without specifying them *(COBOL)*.

COS—Library function giving the cosine of X in radians *(BASIC)*.

COS—Library function giving the cosine of X *(FORTRAN)*.

COS—Library function giving the cosine of X in radians *(Pascal)*.

COSH—Library function giving the hyperbolic cosine of X *(FORTRAN)*.

CSAVE—Command causing program to be saved on a cassette *(BASIC)*.

CURSOR—Statement locating cursor at horizontal point X and vertical point Y *(BASIC)*.

DATA—Used in conjunction with READ to specify data to be input *(BASIC)*.

DATA—Statement used to assign values to variables *(FORTRAN)*.

DATA RECORD—Clause used in a file description to declare names of data records in the file *(COBOL)*.

DECIMAL—Attribute indicating a variable is a number with a decimal point *(PL/1)*.

DECLARE—Statement specifying the attributes of a variable *(PL/1)*.

DEF FN—Defines a user-defined function *(BASIC)*.

DEFINE—Function returning a list of user-defined functions that have been added to the LISP system *(LISP)*.

DEFINED—Attribute indicating a character string is a portion of a larger one or that an array is part of a higher dimension array *(PL/1)*.

DEL—Same as DELETE in some versions of BASIC *(BASIC)*.

DELETE—Command deleting lines in a program *(BASIC)*.

DELETE—Verb removing a record *(COBOL)*.

DIFFERENCE—Function giving the difference in value between two arguments *(LISP)*.

DIM—Command causing space to be allocated in memory for array variables *(BASIC)*.

DIMENSION—Statement setting up an array of variables *(FORTRAN)*.

DISPLAY—Statement used to output literals and other low-volume data *(COBOL)*.

DIV—Operator for division of non-negative integer values, resulting in truncated integer results *(Pascal)*.

DIVIDE—Verb dividing one data item into another *(COBOL)*.

DO—Statement causing an action to be performed *(ALGOL)*.

DO—Used in conjunction with various statements (WHILE, FOR, CASE, etc.) to cause the execution of an action *(Pascal)*.

DO—Statement indicating the start of a sequence of statements which are to be executed in loop fashion *(PL/1)*.

DOUBLE PRECISION—Statement declaring a variable to be a double-precision type *(FORTRAN)*.

DOWNTO—Used in conjunction with FOR to indicate the range over which an operation is performed, starting from a value and decreasing down the range *(Pascal)*.

DSP—Statement causing the printing of a variable and the line number where it is executed *(BASIC)*.

DYNAMIC—Used with ACCESS to indicate a MODE where a file must have indexed organization *(COBOL)*.

EDIT—Command allowing editing of a specific program line *(BASIC)*.

ELSE—Used in conjunction with IF/THEN statements to indicate an alternative to a condition not being met *(ALGOL)*.

ELSE—Used in conjunction with IF to cause execution of a statement when a certain condition is not met *(BASIC)*.

ELSE—Used in conjunction with IF and THEN to indicate a second alternative to a condition *(FORTRAN)*.

ELSE—Used in conjunction with IF to cause the execution of a statement when a certain condition is not met *(Pascal)*.

ELSE—Statement used to create alternative action if a condition is not met *(PL/1)*.

END—Statement ending a sequence of statements *(ALGOL)*.

END—Statement stopping program execution *(BASIC)*.

END—Statement denoting the end of a program *(FORTRAN)*.

END—Used in conjunction with BEGIN to denote the limits of a compound statement or an entire program *(Pascal)*.

END—Statement used to terminate a program or loop *(PL/1)*.

ENDFILE—Statement indicating that the end of a data file has been reached *(FORTRAN)*.

ENTER—Verb allowing more than one language to be used in a COBOL program *(COBOL)*.

ENTIER—Function giving the integer part of an argument *(LISP)*.

EQ—Function returning T if both atoms are identical or NIL if they are not *(LISP)*.

EQUAL—Function returning T if both elements are identical or NIL if they are not *(LISP)*.

EQUIVALENCE—Statement allowing two or more names to be used for the same variable *(FORTRAN)*.

EXAMINE—Verb counting or replacing a character within a data item *(COBOL)*.

EXECUTE—Statement used to cause the execution of a remote programming block *(FORTRAN)*.

EXIT—Verb providing an ending for a program or a group of procedures *(COBOL)*.

EXP—Library function giving value of natural number *e* raised to a specified power *(BASIC)*.

EXP—Library function giving the natural number *e* raised to a specified power *(FORTRAN)*.

EXPT—Function causing one argument to be raised to the power of a second argument *(LISP)*.

EXTERNAL—Statement declaring subprogram names to be used as arguments when calling other subprograms *(FORTRAN)*.

FILE (OF)—Definition used with TYPE to set up a data structure of components of the same type *(Pascal)*.

FILLER—Elementary item of a record that cannot be directly referenced *(COBOL)*.

FIXED—Attribute indicating a variable is written without exponential notation *(PL/1)*.

FLOAT—Library function giving the real form of an integer value *(FORTRAN)*.

FLOAT—Function giving the floating point form of an argument *(LISP)*.

FLOAT—Attribute indicating a variable is in exponential form *(PL/1)*.

FOR—Statement used to indicate beginning point of a repeated action *(ALGOL)*.

FOR—Statement used in conjunction with NEXT to create loop *(BASIC)*.

FOR—Used in conjunction with TO or DO to control the number of times a sequence of operations is performed *(Pascal)*.

FORMAT—Statement used in conjunction with an input or output statement to specify field descriptors *(FORTRAN)*.

FROM—Used to denote the variable, array, or structure that data is transferred out of *(PL/1)*.

FUNCTION—Statement assigning a name to a subroutine and establishing its arguments *(FORTRAN)*.

FUNCTION—Declaration used to identify a set of actions used to compute a pointer or scalar value *(Pascal)*.

GENERATE—Verb causing a report to be produced according to specifications in the report section *(COBOL)*.

GET—Statement used for the input of stream data *(PL/1)*.

GET EDIT—Statement causing data to be input and assigned to variables or rearranged internally *(PL/1)*.

GET STRING . . . EDIT—Statement used to select items from a single character string *(PL/1)*.

GOSUB—Statement causing program to branch to subroutine at specified line number *(BASIC)*.

GO TO—Statement causing program control to shift to point indicated by a label *(ALGOL)*.

GO TO—Verb shifting program control to another part of the program *(COBOL)*.

GO TO—Statement transferring control to another line number *(FORTRAN)*.

GO TO—Unconditional statement transferring program to a labeled statement *(PL/1)*.

GOTO—Statement causing control to shift to a specific line number *(BASIC)*.

GOTO—Used with a statement label to shift the program control to another statement in the program *(Pascal)*.

IABS—Library function giving the absolute value of an integer *(FORTRAN)*.

IF—Expression used in conjunction with THEN and sometimes ELSE to make execution of statements dependent upon a condition being met *(ALGOL, BASIC)*.

IF—Verb used with THEN and ELSE to indicate a condition and its consequences *(COBOL)*.

IF—Statement causing another statement to be executed depending upon a condition *(FORTRAN)*.

IF—Used in conjunction with THEN or ELSE to make execution of a statement conditional upon a certain condition *(Pascal)*.

IF—Statement used with THEN to perform some action if a condition is met *(PL/1)*.

IMPLICIT—Statement declaring all variables beginning with the same letter to be of the same type *(FORTRAN)*.

IN—Operator used to indicate whether a value is a member of a set *(Pascal)*.

INARRAY—Primitive procedure causing an array of real values to be input *(ALGOL)*.

INDEX—Statement indicating that a data item is an index type *(COBOL)*.

INDEX—Function of two character strings giving a FIXED BINARY value of 0 if the second string is not a substring of the first; otherwise, the value is the position in bytes where the second string begins to appear as a substring of the first string *(PL/1)*.

ININTEGER—Primitive procedure causing integer values to be input *(ALGOL)*.

INITIAL—Used with DECLARE to set the values of variables *(PL/1)*.

INP—Reads a byte from a port specified by an integer expression in the range 0 through 255 *(BASIC)*.

INPUT—Enters data into memory and assigns it to variables following INPUT *(BASIC)*.

INPUT—Verb causing data to be entered into a COBOL program *(COBOL)*.

INPUT—Attribute specifying that a file is to be used only for input into memory *(PL/1)*.

INREAL—Primitive procedure causing a real value to be input *(ALGOL)*.

ISIGN—Library function transferring the sign of one integer value to another *(FORTRAN)*.

INSPECT—Verb counting or replacing a character within a data item *(COBOL)*.

INSYMBOL—Primitive procedure causing alphanumeric data to be input *(ALGOL)*.

INT—Library function giving integer portion of an expression that is less than or equal to the expression *(BASIC)*.

INT—Library function converting a real value to an integer value *(FORTRAN)*.

INTARRAY—Primitive procedure causing an array of integer values to be input *(ALGOL)*.

INTEGER—Declaration denoting a variable contains only integer values *(ALGOL)*.

INTEGER—Statement declaring a variable to be an integer *(FORTRAN)*.

INTEGER—Variable type whose values are all whole numbers *(Pascal)*.

INTERSECTION—Function giving the intersection of the objects in two sets *(LISP)*.

INITIATE—Verb causing the start of report processing *(COBOL)*.

INTO—Used to denote the variable, array, or structure that data is input to *(PL/1)*.

JUSTIFIED—Clause that gives the positioning of data within a data item *(COBOL)*.

LABEL—Assigns a statement label number to a statement *(Pascal)*.

LABEL—Variable type with a label as a value *(PL/1)*.

LABEL RECORD—Clause indicating whether there are any label records in a file description *(COBOL)*.

LAMBDA—Construction doing away with the requirement for defining new function names *(LISP)*.

LAST—Function returning the last element of a list *(LISP)*.

LEADING—Description of the leftmost character in a string *(COBOL)*.

LEFT$—Function allowing movement of characters from the left end of a string into another string *(BASIC)*.

LEN—Function returning the full length of a string *(BASIC)*.

LENGTH—Function giving the number of elements in the first line of a list *(LISP)*.

LENGTH—Function giving a FIXED BINARY value equal to the number of characters in a character string *(PL/1)*.

LET—Statement assigning a value to a variable *(BASIC)*.

LINE-COUNTER—Special register for each report description found in the report section of data division *(COBOL)*.

LINE INPUT—Statement allowing printing of a prompting message and inputting of a string *(BASIC)*.

LIST—Function giving a list of the values of a group of arguments *(LISP)*.

LIST—Command causing the listing of the lines in a program *(BASIC)*.

LOCK—Verb ending file processing *(COBOL)*.

MAP—Function that applies the value of a function to all elements of a list *(LISP)*.

MAX—Function returning the largest value of a group of arguments *(LISP)*.

MAX0—Library function giving the largest of two or more integer values *(FORTRAN)*.

MAX1—Library function giving the largest of two or more real values, with the result converted to integer form *(FORTRAN)*.

MEMSET—Function returning T if an object is a member of a particular set *(LISP)*.

MERGE—Verb combining two or more files *(COBOL)*.

MID$—Function allowing movement of characters from the middle of one string to another *(BASIC)*.

MIN—Function giving the smallest value of a group of arguments *(LISP)*.

MINUS—Function giving the negative value of an argument *(LISP)*.

MIN0—Library function giving the smallest of two or more integer values *(FORTRAN)*.

MIN1—Library function giving the smallest of two or more real values with the result converted to integer form *(FORTRAN)*.

MOD—Operator giving the remainder of a division *(BASIC)*.

MOD—Library function giving the remainder of an integer division *(FORTRAN)*.

MOD—Operator giving the remainder for division of integer values *(Pascal)*.

MOVE—Verb transferring data to other data items *(COBOL)*.

MULTIPLY—Verb multiplying two data items *(COBOL)*.

NAMELIST—Statement allowing input and output of several variables without a FORMAT statement by calling one name *(FORTRAN)*.

NEW—Deletes current program and clears all variables *(BASIC)*.

NEXT—Used in conjunction with FOR to create loop *(BASIC)*.

NIL—The empty list; also frequently used to end a list *(LISP)*.

NOT—Logical operator negating a statement or operand *(COEOL)*.

NOT—Boolean operator indicating the expression is true if one element of the expression is not true *(Pascal)*.

NOTE—Verb indicating that the material, which follows, is a comment *(COBOL)*.

NOTRACE—Same as TROFF in some versions of BASIC *(BASIC)*.

OCCURS—Clause indicating subscripts of data items *(COBOL)*.

OF—Used in conjunction with CASE to indicate alternatives according to different values of an expression *(Pascal)*.

ON—Used in conjunction with GOSUB and GOTO to cause program to move to a specific line *(BASIC)*.

ON ENDFILE—Statement specifying instructions to be executed when an "end of file" mark is found by a READ statement *(PL/1)*.

OPEN—Verb making files available for processing *(COBOL)*.

OPEN—Statement which specifies a file is set to input or output data *(PL/1)*.

OR—Logical operator indicating statement is true if either expression is true *(BASIC)*.

OR—Function returning a T if either argument is T, or NIL if both arguments are NIL *(LISP)*.

OR—Boolean operator indicating the expression is true if either element of the expression is true *(Pascal)*.

ORGANIZATION—Clause indicating whether a file is organized in sequential, relative, or indexed form *(COBOL)*.

OUT—Statement causing byte specified by a second expression to be sent to port specified by the first expression, values of both expressions must be in range 0 through 255 *(BASIC)*.

OUTARRAY—Primitive procedure causing an array of real values to be output *(ALGOL)*.

OUTINTEGER—Primitive procedure causing an integer to be output *(ALGOL)*.

OUTPUT—Attribute specifying that a file is to be used only for output of data from memory *(PL/1)*.

OUTREAL—Primitive procedure causing the value of a real variable to be output in floating-point form *(ALGOL)*.

OUTSTRING—Primitive procedure causing literals to be output *(ALGOL)*.

OUTSYMBOL—Primtive procedure causing alphanumeric data to be output *(ALGOL)*.

OUTTARRAY—Primitive procedure causing an array of integer values to be output *(ALGOL)*.

PACKED ARRAY—Similar to ARRAY, but instructs the compiler that storage should be economized, at the cost of inefficiency in being accessed *(Pascal)*.

PACKED RECORD—Similar to RECORD, but instructs the compiler that storage should be economized at the cost of some inefficiency when being accessed *(Pascal)*.

PAGE—Clause that defines length of a page and its vertical subdivisions *(COBOL)*.

PAUSE—Statement causing program execution to temporarily pause and a message to be printed *(FORTRAN)*.

PEEK—Function reading the value of a memory location specified by an expression *(BASIC)*.

PERFORM—Verb transferring program control to specified paragraph *(COBOL)*.

PICTURE—Clause describing a data item *(COBOL)*.

PICTURE—Specification used to describe a character string in which character is restricted to an indicated type *(PL/1)*.

PLUS—Function adding together the values of a group of arguments *(LISP)*.

POKE—Statement causing byte specified by a second expression to be stored in a location specified by the first expression *(BASIC)*.

POS—Gives a number indicating current cursor position on video display *(BASIC)*.

PRINT—Statement outputting data specified by a variable or literal *(BASIC)*.

PRINT—Statement causing a variable or literal to be output *(FORTRAN)*.

PRINT—Function causing an element to be sent to an output device *(LISP)*.

PRINT @—Statement causing printing at a specified position *(BASIC)*.

PRINT USING—Statement specifying PRINT format *(BASIC)*.

PROCEDURE—Statement assigning a name to a group of statements *(ALGOL)*.

PROCEDURE—Declaration defining part of a program and giving it an identifier that is used to call it *(Pascal)*.

PROCEDURE—Follows name of and identifies subprograms or subroutines of main program *(PL/1)*.

PROCEDURE OPTIONS (MAIN)—First line in program; follows program name *(PL/1)*.

PROCEED—Verb changing point in a program where GO TO shifts control *(COBOL)*.

PROG—Function consisting of a list of variables followed by a list of arguments *(LISP)*.

PROGRAM—Heading denoting the beginning of a program, including program name and the parameters by which the program communicates with its environment *(Pascal)*.

PUT—Statement used for output of stream data *(PL/1)*.

PUT EDIT—Statement causing data to be either output through an output device or rearranged internally *(PL/1)*.

PUT STRING . . . EDIT—Statement used to combine several items into a single string *(PL/1)*.

QUOTE—Constant with a value of one or more quotation characters *(COBOL)*.

QUOTE—Function returning the exact value of an argument *(LISP)*.

QUOTIENT—Function dividing one argument by another *(LISP)*.

RANDOM—Used with ACCESS to indicate a MODE where a file must have indexed organization *(COBOL)*.

READ—Statement assigning values in DATA statement to numbers or string variables *(BASIC)*.

READ—Verb moving a record from a file and making it available for processing *(COBOL)*.

READ—Statement causing data to be input *(FORTRAN)*.

READ—Function causing an element to be read into a system from an input device *(LISP)*.

READ—Statement used to input data to assign values to variables *(Pascal)*.

READ—Statement used to transfer record-oriented data from external memory into the computer *(PL/1)*.

READLN—Statement which reads data in a manner similar to READ but which causes a skip to the next line of data *(Pascal)*.

REAL—Declaration denoting a variable contains real number values *(ALGOL)*.

REAL—Statement declaring a variable to be a real value *(FORTRAN)*.

REAL—Type of variables whose values are real numbers. This type of variable can generally accept whole numbers as well *(Pascal)*.

REAL—Attribute indicating a variable is a real number *(PL/1)*.

RECIP—Function giving the reciprocal of an argument *(LISP)*.

RECORD—Structure type consisting of a fixed number of components that may be of different types *(Pascal)*.

RECORD CONTAINS—Clause in the file description specifying size of data records *(COBOL)*.

RECURSIVE—Identifies procedure that is recursive; i.e., it can call itself *(PL/1)*.

REDEFINES—Clause allowing a second data name to define a storage area *(COBOL)*.

RELEASE—Verb transferring records to the first sequence of SORT action *(COBOL)*.

RENAMES—Clause giving alternative groupings of elementary items *(COBOL)*.

REPEAT—Used in conjunction with UNTIL to indicate that an action is to be repeated until the expression following UNTIL is true *(Pascal)*.

REM—Nonexecutable statement for program clarity and user convenience *(BASIC)*.

REMARKS—Clause indicating a comment follows *(COBOL)*.

REN—Same as RENUM in some versions of BASIC *(BASIC)*.

RENUM—Command renumbering lines in a program to allow insertion of new lines *(BASIC)*.

REPORT—Clause used to name reports in the report file *(COBOL)*.

REPORT SECTION—Part of data division that contains report descriptions *(COBOL)*.

RERUN—Clause specifying when and where rerun information is recorded *(COBOL)*.

RESERVE—Clause specifying the number of input/output areas allocated to a file *(COBOL)*.

RESET—Standard procedure allowing file scanning *(Pascal)*.

RESTORE—Statement allowing data in DATA statements to be re-read *(BASIC)*.

RESUME—Command causing program execution to resume at a specific line *(BASIC)*.

RETURN—Statement causing program to branch to statement following last GOSUB *(BASIC)*.

RETURN—Verb getting records from last phase of MERGE and SORT actions *(COBOL)*.

RETURN—Statement transferring execution from a subroutine to the main program *(FORTRAN)*.

RETURN—Statement in a procedure causing a return to the calling program *(PL/1)*.

RETURNS—Statement specifying the attributes for the form of a value produced by a procedure *(PL/1)*.

REVERSE—Function causing the objects in a list to be reversed *(LISP)*.

REWRITE—Discards sequence currently associated with a file and allows it to receive a new sequence *(Pascal)*.

RIGHT$—Function allowing movement of characters from the right end of a string into another string *(BASIC)*.

RND—Function returning a random number between 0 and 1 *(BASIC)*.

ROUNDED—Clause causing a result to be rounded to the nearest least-significant digit *(COBOL)*.

RUN—Command starting execution of a program. If a line number is given, execution starts at specified line *(BASIC)*.

RUN—Follows STOP to end program execution *(COBOL)*.

SAME—Clause causing two or more files to share the same area during processing *(COBOL)*.

SCRATCH—Deletes current program and clears all variables. Used instead of NEW in some systems *(BASIC)*.

SEARCH—Verb that scans a table for a data item meeting specified conditions *(COBOL)*.

SECURITY—Paragraph in identification division that can be followed by a comment *(COBOL)*.

SEGMENT-LINE—Clause varying the number of permanent segments in a program *(COBOL)*.

SELECT—Clause associating a file with an external file; used in conjunction with ASSIGN *(COBOL)*.

SET—Statement assigning values to index data items *(COBOL)*.

SET (OF)—Definition establishing a set of objects of the same type *(Pascal)*.

SETQ—Function with an alpha atom and an argument which gives the alpha atom the value of the argument *(LISP)*.

SGN—Function returning the sign (positive or negative) of an expression *(BASIC)*.

SIGN—Library function transferring the sign of one real value to another *(FORTRAN)*.

SIN—Library function giving the sine of an expression *(BASIC)*.

SIN—Library function giving the sine of a real value *(FORTRAN)*.

SINH—Library function giving the hyperbolic sine of a real value *(FORTRAN)*.

SKIP—Statement causing the input or output to skip to the next record *(PL/1)*.

SORT—Verb creating a sort file that sorts records and makes them available in sorted order *(COBOL.)*

SOURCE—Clause used in a report to identify data item moved to a printable item *(COBOL)*.

SOURCE-COMPUTER—Paragraph in the environment division describing computer on which program is compiled *(COBOL)*.

SPACE—Constant representing the space character *(COBOL)*.

SPACE$—Function giving a string of spaces whose length is specified by the expression which follows *(BASIC)*.

SQR—Library function giving square root of an expression *(BASIC)*.

SQRT—Library function giving the square root of X *(FORTRAN)*.

SQRT—Function giving the absolute value of an argument *(LISP)*.

STEP—Statement indicating how the beginning value of a repeated action is increased *(ALGOL)*.

STEP—Used with FOR/NEXT loop to indicate increments in which loop travels over a range of values *(BASIC)*.

STOP—Statement stopping program execution *(BASIC)*.

STOP—Verb used with literal to temporarily end execution of a program *(COBOL)*.

STOP—Statement causing the execution of a program to stop *(FORTRAN)*.

STRING—Function combining elements of an array or structure into a single string *(PL/1)*

STR$—Function giving a string representation of an expression *(BASIC)*.

SUBROUTINE—Statement assigning a name to a self-contained program *(FORTRAN)*.

SUBSTR—Function defining a substring of a string along with its number of characters and the letter of the string where substring begins *(PL/1)*.

SUB1—Function subtracting one from the value of an argument *(LISP)*.

SUBTRACT—Verb subtracting one data item from another *(COBOL)*.

SUM—Clause setting up a sum counter in a report group description and designating data items summed into the counter *(COBOL)*.

SWAP—Statement causing the value of two variables to be exchanged *(BASIC)*.

SWITCH—Declaration causing program control to shift to labeled points depending upon the value of an index variable *(ALGOL)*.

SYNCHRONIZED—Clause specifying how elementary data items are stored *(COBOL)*.

SYSTEM—Statement allowing loading of machine language programs and data *(BASIC)*.

TAB—Function causing spacing to horizontal position indicated *(BASIC)*.

TALLY—Special register used in conjunction with EXAMINE *(COBOL)*.

TAN—Function giving the tangent of an expression in radians *(BASIC)*.

TAN—Library function giving the tangent of X *(FORTRAN)*.

TANH—Library function giving the hyperbolic tangent of X *(FORTRAN)*.

TERMINATE—Verb causing report processing to be completed *(COBOL)*.

THEN—Used in conjunction with IF to indicate consequence of a condition *(ALGOL)*.

THEN—Used in conjunction with IF to cause execution of a statement when specified condition is met *(BASIC)*.

THEN—Used in conjunction with IF to indicate a consequence for a condition *(FORTRAN)*.

THEN—Used in conjunction with IF to cause the execution of a statement when a condition is met *(Pascal)*.

THEN—Used in conjunction with IF for a conditionally executed action *(PL/1)*.

TIMES—Function multiplying several arguments *(LISP)*.

TO—Used in conjunction with FOR to indicate the range over which an operation is performed *(Pascal)*.

TO—Indicates ending index for a DO loop *(PL/1)*.

TRACE—Same as TRON in some versions of BASIC *(BASIC)*.

TRACE—Function showing the different arguments another function takes and their values *(LISP)*.

TRANSLATE—Function that replaces individual characters in a string with other characters *(PL/1)*.

TROFF—Statement turning off trace function activated by TRON *(BASIC)*.

TRON—Activates trace function giving line number of each line as it is executed to illustrate program flow *(BASIC)*.

TYPE—Clause in the report group description specifying the particular type of report group *(COBOL)*.

TYPE—Statement used on some systems in place of PRINT *(FORTRAN)*.

TYPE—Declaration allowing definition of value types other than real, integer, or Boolean *(Pascal)*.

UNION—Function resulting in the union of the objects of two sets *(LISP)*.

UNTIL—Statement indicating the ending point of a repeated action *(ALGOL)*.

UNTIL—Used in conjunction with REPEAT to indicate an action is repeated until the expression following UNTIL is true *(Pascal)*.

UNTRACE—Function whose argument is a list of function names that will no longer be TRACEd *(LISP)*.

UPDATE—Attribute specifying that a file can be used for both input and output from memory *(PL/1)*.

USAGE—Clause specifying manner in which a data item is represented in storage *(COBOL)*.

USR—Function allowing calling of machine language subroutine *(BASIC)*.

VAL—Function returning numerical value of a string *(BASIC)*.

VALUE—Declaration that a parameter is to be transferred by value instead of by name *(ALGOL)*.

VALUE IS—Clause defining value of constants *(COBOL)*.

VALUE OF—Clause giving a certain value to a data item in the label record of a file *(COBOL)*.

VAR—Declaration giving a list of identifiers denoting new variables and their types *(Pascal)*.

VARPTR—Function giving memory address of a variable and its value *(BASIC)*.

VARYING—Attribute indicating the length of a character string will change during program execution *(PL/1)*.

VERIFY—Function that searches a string for a character not in a second string *(PL/1)*.

WAIT—Statement of first port is joined with second port by AND and joined with third port by XOR, causing program to stop and await a nonzero result *(BASIC)*.

WHILE—Statement indicating an action is to be performed so long as a certain condition is being met *(ALGOL)*.

WHILE—Statement causing execution of a loop or another statement as long as a condition is met *(FORTRAN)*.

WHILE—Used in conjunction with DO to perform an action as long as a controlling statement is true *(Pascal)*.

WHILE—Statement indicating a loop is performed as long as a condition is met *(PL/1)*.

WIDTH—Command setting the width in characters of a printing terminal line *(BASIC)*.

WITH—Statement enabling access to the components of a record as though they were simple variables *(Pascal)*.

WRITE—Verb producing printout of a record *(COBOL)*.

WRITE—Statement causing output in specified field descriptors *(FORTRAN)*.

WRITE—Statement causing expressions to be output together *(Pascal)*.

WRITE—Statement used to transfer record-oriented data from the computer to external memory *(PL/1)*.

WRITELN—Statement causing expressions to be output on a single line *(Pascal)*.

XOR—Logical operator causing statement to be true if both elements are different from each other *(BASIC)*.

ZERO—Constant representing the value or character 0 *(COBOL)*.

ZEROP—Function resulting in T if argument is zero, NIL if value is not zero *(LISP)*.

TO THE READER

Sams Computer books cover Fundamentals — Programming — Interfacing — Technology written to meet the needs of computer engineers, professionals, scientists, technicians, students, educators, business owners, personal computerists and home hobbyists.

Our Tradition is to meet your needs and in so doing we invite you to tell us what your needs and interests are by completing the following:

1. I need books on the following topics:

_____

_____

_____

_____

_____

_____

2. I have the following Sams titles:

_____

_____

_____

_____

_____

_____

3. My occupation is:

_____ Scientist, Engineer   _____ D P Professional

_____ Personal computerist   _____ Business owner

_____ Technician, Serviceman   _____ Computer store owner

_____ Educator   _____ Home hobbyist

_____ Student   Other _____

_____

Name (print) _____

Address _____

City _____ State _____ Zip _____

Mail to: **Howard W. Sams & Co., Inc.**
Marketing Dept. #CBS1/80
4300 W. 62nd St., P.O. Box 7092
Indianapolis, Indiana 46206